Footprint Handbook

St Lucia &
Don

SARAH CAME

This is
St Lucia &
Dominica

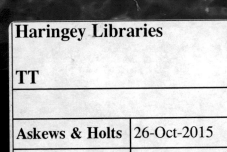

St Lucia, Dominica and Martinique are part of the Windward Island chain, a series of volcanic peaks jutting out of the sea. They form a barrier between the Atlantic Ocean and the Caribbean Sea and all have a wild, blustery east coast and a calm, sheltered west coast with lovely natural harbours and picturesque fishing villages. Sulphur fumaroles and hot springs are evidence of the dormant, but not dead, volcanoes, while the volcanic soil provides immense fertility. There are large areas of lush rainforest with national parks protecting places of biodiversity or natural beauty on land and underwater. The islands are a haven for birds with lots of endemic species, while the sea is teeming with fish and other marine life including whales and dolphins. Hikers and birdwatchers are spoilt for choice, with many rewarding trails through forested mountains, following rivers and along beaches. There is always something to do and an action-packed holiday can include any number of watersports, such as canyoning, kayaking, diving and snorkelling.

These islands were all at one time colonized by the French and share a cultural heritage even though St Lucia and Dominica eventually became British before getting their independence. Martinique has remained French and is a part of France: a Département. Imported African slaves brought to work on plantations have added to the rich ethnic mix. This Caribbean melting pot of races and cultures has produced a language known as Kwéyòl, which is widely spoken, with regional differences. St Lucia and Dominica have retained French names for many of their towns and villages, where the older colonial buildings are decorated with gingerbread fretwork and jalousie shutters. They share a Créole cuisine, Roman Catholicism, and music, with Cadence, Zouk, Compas, Bouyou and Soukous heard at Créole festivals and fêtes around the islands. However, the official language is English, cars drive on the left and cricket is the most popular sport.

Sarah Cameron

Best of
St Lucia &
Dominica

top things to do and see

❶ Castries market

Castries market is a hive of activity, especially when a cruise ship is in town. It's a wonderful place to shop for tropical fruits and vegetables, as well as a staggering array of spices, including enormous chunks of cinnamon bark and shiny brown nutmegs, traditional coal pots and other souvenirs. Page 31.

❷ Grand Anse turtle watching

The long windy beach at Grand Anse in the north of the island is one of the Caribbean's most important nesting sites for the world's largest turtle – the majestic leatherback. From March to July it's possible to witness the enormous reptiles hauling themselves up the sand to lay their eggs. Page 40.

❸ Maria Islands

These two tiny islands, across from Anse de Sable Beach, are a nature reserve and a popular day trip. Home to the rare racer snake, colourful ground lizard and various nesting seabirds, there's a good beach on the leeward side and the coral reefs offshore are great for snorkelling. Page 47.

❹ The Pitons

When you hear the words 'St Lucia', an image of the Pitons will most likely spring to mind; the twin volcanic peaks are the most photographed landmark on the island. Rising like skyscrapers out of the sea, the ancient forest-clad plugs are a majestic backdrop for the charming town of Soufrière. Page 54.

❺ Edmond Forest hiking and birdwatching

Deep in a tropical nature reserve at the heart of the island, a hiking trail leads through lush rainforest, abundant with orchids, strangler figs and indigenous birds, such as the endangered St Lucia parrot. With tantalizing glimpses of the sea and the island's highest peak, it's an enjoyable way to experience the forest. Page 54.

❻ Boiling Lake

Part of the Morne Trois Pitons National Park in Dominica's mountainous volcanic interior, a rigorous hike through the Valley of Desolation brings you to the second largest boiling lake in the world. Like a cauldron of bubbling milky-blue water, it's often enveloped in a cloud of vapour giving it an otherworldly feel. Page 92.

❼ Titou Gorge canyoning

Carved out of volcanic rock over millions of years, Dominica's rugged interior is ideal for canyoning. Wading through rivers, rappelling down rock faces or jumping from cascades are a great way to explore the depths of the island. At Titou Gorge, a narrow gorge and a waterfall offer an exciting introduction to the sport. Page 93.

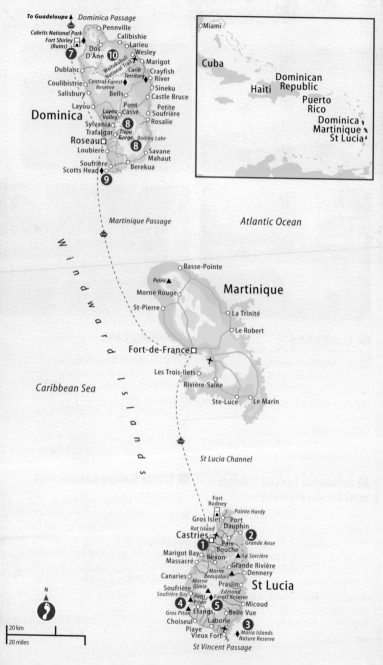

To Guadeloupe
Dominica Passage

Cabrits National Park
Fort Shirley
(Ruins)
7
Pennville
Calibishie
Dos
D'Âne
10
Larieu
Wesley
Marigot
Crayfish
River
Sineku
Castle Bruce
Dublanc
Coulibistrie
Central Forest
Reserve
Bells
Salisbury
Layou
Layou
Valley
Pont
Cassé
Petite
Soufrière
Rosalie
Sylvania
8
Dominica
Trafalgar
Titou
Gorge
Boiling Lake
Roseau
8
Loubière
Savane
Mahaut
Soufrière
9
Berekua
Scotts Head

Waitukubuli
National Trail
Carib
Territory

Martinique Passage

Atlantic Ocean

W i n d w a r d
I s l a n d s

Basse-Pointe
Pelée
Morne Rouge
Martinique
St-Pierre
La Trinité
Le Robert
Fort-de-France
Les Trois-Îlets
Rivière-Salée
Caribbean Sea
Ste-Luce
Le Marin

St Lucia Channel

Fort
Rodney
Pointe Hardy
Gros Islet
Port
Rat Island
Dauphin
Castries
2
Paix
Bouche
Grande Anse
Marigot Bay
Bexon
La Sorcière
Massacré
Grande Rivière
Canaries
Morne
Beaujolais
Dennery
Morne
Gimie
Praslin
Soufrière
Edmond
Forest Reserve
St Lucia
Soufrière Bay
Petit
Piton
4
5
Micoud
Gros Piton
Etangs
Belle Vue
Choiseul
Laborie
3
Piaye
Maria Islands
Nature Reserve
Vieux Fort
St Vincent Passage

Miami
Cuba
Dominican
Republic
Haiti
Puerto
Rico
Dominica
Martinique
St Lucia

N

20 km
20 miles

8 Soufrière and Scotts Head

This marine reserve off the south coast of Dominica is the most picturesque bay on the island both above and below the water. Characterized by warm underwater sulphur vents and abrupt coral reef drop-offs, it's a site for pelagic fish and cetaceans including spinner dolphins and sperm whales. Page 94.

9 Fort Shirley, Cabrits Peninsula

A former military outpost on a scenic peninsula in the north of the island, Fort Shirley is Dominica's most important historic site. The 18th-century British garrison once housed more than 600 soldiers. Some of the ruins have been rebuilt, while others lie half-buried in the jungle and are fun to explore. Page 96.

10 Waitukubuli National Trail

This coast-to-coast hiking trail winds its way for 115 miles through lush virgin rainforest, over steep mountainous ridges, past waterfalls, coastal villages and down to the sea again. It's a showcase of Dominica's rich cultural and natural heritage and can be completed as a series of day hikes. Page 112.

Scotts Head fishermen, Dominica

Route planner

A weekend

If you only have a couple of days to spare on St Lucia, you should try and take in Friday evening activities, with the fish fry at **Anse La Raye** or the jump-up at **Gros Islet**. Both are street parties where the food and booze are in abundance and having a good time is guaranteed. **Rodney Bay** is probably the best area to base yourself for a weekend, with the beach, watersports, restaurants, bars and clubs all within walking distance. If you have the time, do a day trip to **Soufrière** and the **Pitons**; most excursions start from the marina or pick up at hotels in the area.

On Dominica, you will probably want to do something active on your short trip, such as a day's diving, hiking in the mountains, canyoning or whale watching. The dive lodges on the west coast at **Castle Comfort** are convenient and within easy reach of bars and restaurants. Alternatively, **Portsmouth** in the northwest is closer to the airport, the beaches are better and the university students there create a relatively lively nightlife.

If you are travelling between the two islands by ferry, Martinique is your stopover and a night in **Fort-de-France** can be fun, with a selection of excellent restaurants to while away the evening over Créole food washed down with a bottle of good French wine.

A week or more

St Lucia is a small volcanic island just 238 square miles, but, with a mountainous spine, if you don't want to be driving on mountain roads all the time, consider a two-centre holiday. You could divide your time between the activities of **Rodney Bay**, in the northwest, and the peace of a country area with the forest at your doorstep in the southwest, around **Soufrière**. Dominica, a similarly shaped teardrop island of only 290 square miles, is even more mountainous and again, it would be worth dividing your time between the north and the south to enjoy all the attractions this tiny country has to offer. A walk in the rainforest is not to be missed: the views are spectacular, with majestic mountains, steep valleys and endless shades of green, where you will be serenaded by a huge variety of birds, frogs and other creatures of the forest. A tour to see the leatherback turtles laying their eggs on **Grand Anse Beach** on St Lucia or **Rosalie Bay** on Dominica is a must, as is a whale-watching trip. There are about 20 species of whale and dolphin in the waters around both islands. Diving and snorkelling is rewarding off the leeward coasts, with the added attraction of underwater springs off the coast of Dominica.

It is well worth making the ferry journey between the two islands, dividing your holiday between St Lucia and Dominica. International flight connections are better to St Lucia, so start and finish there. Martinique lies between the two and a stopover in Fort-de-France is required one way, but the return can be done in one go. There are flights if you prefer, but the scenic benefits of the ferry are well worth the extra time. For details of Express des Iles services, see page 132.

ON THE ROAD
Best activities

- **Birdwatching** in the Edmund Forest, deep in the tropical nature reserve, page 55.

- **Canyoning** in Titou Gorge where a narrow channel ends in a torrential waterfall, page 93.

- **Diving** in the marine park at Soufrière; a pristine underworld adventure, page 51.

- **Diving** or **snorkelling** off Soufrière and Scott's Head, swimming through the bubbles of underwater hot springs at a site known as Champagne, page 94.

- **Hiking** some or all of the Waitukubuli National Trail, taking in Dominica's dense forests, volcanic hills, rivers and waterfalls, page 112.

- **Kiteboarding** or **windsurfing** at Anse de Sables, where wind conditions are exciting but you won't get carried out to the ocean, page 47.

- **Sailing** from Rodney Bay down the west coast for a view of the cliffs, forests and majestic Pitons, page 76.

- **Turtle watching** on Grand Anse, an overnight vigil of the leatherbacks hauling themselves up the sand to lay their eggs, page 42.

- **Watching a Test Match** at St Lucia's Beausejour Cricket Ground, one of the best pitches in the West Indies, page 73.

- **Whale watching** in Soufrière Bay with playful dolphins leaping in and out of your wake, page 114.

When to go

… and when not to

Climate

The climate is tropical. The volcanic mountains and forests of St Lucia, Dominica and Martinique attract more rain than some other, more low-lying islands in the Caribbean. The driest and coolest time of year is usually December-April, coinciding with the winter peak in tourism as those from Europe and the US escape to the sun. However, there can be showers, which keep things green. Temperatures can fall to 20°C during the day, depending on altitude, but are normally in the high 20s, tempered by cooling trade winds. The mean annual temperature is about 26°C. At other times of the year the temperature rises only slightly, but greater humidity can make it feel hotter if you are away from the coast, where the northeast trade winds are a cooling influence. The main climate hazard is hurricane season (See page 12), which runs from June to November. Tropical storms can cause flooding and mudslides, the latest being Tropical Storm Erica which battered Dominica at the end of August 2015.

Festivals

You can time your visit to coincide with one of the islands' festivals. On St Lucia, **Carnival** is celebrated in July with colourful parades and pageants, music and competitions; visitors are welcome to join in. Dominica's carnival, which takes place in February/March, is one of the friendliest in the Caribbean and is a celebration of calypso, building up to two days of street jump-up. The greatest influx of visitors is usually for St Lucia's annual **Jazz Festival** in May, when open-air concerts by internationally renowned artists are held around the island. In October, Dominica hosts the **World Créole Music Festival** attracting artists from across the globe. Other events to consider are **Test Matches**, when cricket fans travel to support their team, or the arrival of the **Atlantic Rally for Cruisers** in the first week of December, when Rodney Bay on St Lucia fills with yachts and their crew, hell-bent on enjoying themselves on terra firma. For further details, see page 70 for St Lucia's festivals and page 109 for those in Dominica.

June too soon, July stand by, August it must, September remember,
October all over

In recent years there have been several late storms and the 'October all over' has proved a myth. There was little hurricane activity in the region from the 1950s until the late 1980s. Many of the islands were not affected by hurricanes and residents thought little of them. Homes were not built to withstand severe storms. In 1989 this all started to change when several violent storms roared through the islands and Hurricane Hugo did untold damage in the US Virgin Islands. The next few years were relatively quiet but 1995 struck with a bang (three names were 'retired' in deference to the dead and injured) and was the start of a 10-year period that has gone down in history as the most active stretch on record for hurricanes. Analysts expect that this active hurricane era will last another two or three decades.

In the daily weather forecasts, a **tropical depression** is an organized system of clouds and thunderstorms with a defined circulation and maximum sustained winds of 38 mph (33 knots) or less; a **tropical storm** is an organized system of strong thunderstorms with a defined circulation and maximum sustained winds of 39-73 mph (34-63 knots); a **hurricane** is an intense tropical weather system with a well-defined circulation and maximum sustained winds of 74 mph (64 knots) or more.

A hurricane develops in warm waters and air, which is why the tropics are known for hurricanes. Powered by heat from the sea they are steered by the easterly trade winds and the temperate westerly winds, as well as their own ferocious energy. In the Atlantic, these storms form off the African coast and move west, developing as they come into warmer water. Around the core, winds grow to great velocity, generating violent seas. The process by which a disturbance forms and strengthens into a hurricane depends on at least three conditions: warm water, moisture and wind pattern near the ocean surface that spirals air inward. Bands of thunderstorms form and allow the air to warm further and rise higher into the atmosphere. If the winds at these higher levels are light, the structure remains intact and allows for further strengthening. If the winds are strong, they will shear off the top and stop the development. If the system develops, a definite eye is formed around which the most violent activity takes place; this is known as the eyewall. The centre of the eye is relatively calm. When the eye passes over land those on the ground are often misled that the hurricane is over; some even abandon safe shelter, not aware that as the eye passes the other side of the eyewall will produce violent winds and the other half of the hurricane. At the top of the eyewall (around 50,000 ft), most of the air is propelled outward, increasing the air's upward motion. Some of the air however, moves inward and sinks into the eye and creates a cloud-free area.

The word 'hurricane' is derived from the Amerindian 'Hurakan', both the Carib god of evil and also one of the Maya creator gods who blew his breath across the chaotic water and brought forth dry land. In the north Atlantic, Gulf of Mexico, Caribbean and the eastern Pacific they are called hurricanes, in Australia, cyclones or 'willy willy', and in the Philippines, 'baguio'. In the Western North Pacific tropical cyclones of hurricane force are called typhoons. The first time hurricanes were named was by an Australian forecaster in the early 1900s who called them after political figures he disliked. During the Second World War US Army forecasters named storms after their girlfriends and wives. Between 1950 and 1952 they were given phonetic names (Able, Baker, Charlie). In 1953 the Weather Bureau started giving them female names again. Today individual names (male and female) are chosen by the National Hurricane Center in Miami (www.nhc.noaa.gov) and submitted to the World Meteorology Organization in Geneva, Switzerland. If approved these become the official names for the upcoming hurricane season. As a system develops, it is assigned a name in alphabetical order from the official list.

There is very good information before hurricanes hit any land, thanks to accurate weather data gathered by the Hurricane Hunters from Keesler Airforce Base in the USA. During the storm season they operate out of St Croix in the US Virgin Islands, where they are closer to storms. This elite group of men and women actually fly through the eye of a hurricane in C130 airplanes gathering critical information on the wind speeds and directions and other data. This is sent to the Miami Hurricane Center where a forecast is made and sent to all islands in the potential path so they can prepare for the storm. Most of the island governments are now well prepared to cope with hurricanes and have disaster relief teams in place, while many of the island resorts, especially the larger ones, have their own generators and water supplies.

Essential hurricanes

When potentially violent weather is approaching, the local met office issues advisories:

Tropical storm watch Be on alert for a storm (winds of 39-73 mph) which may pose threats to coastal areas within 36 hours.

Tropical storm warning The storm is expected within 24 hours.

Hurricane watch Hurricane conditions could be coming in 36 hours.

Hurricane warning The hurricane is expected within 24 hours.

While a hurricane can certainly pose a threat to life, in most cases if precautions are taken the risks are reduced. Some of the main hazards are storm surge, heavy winds and rains. There is usually disruption of services such as communications, internal transport and airline services. Ideally, if a hurricane is approaching, it is better for the tourist to evacuate the island. During the hurricane, which is usually six to 36 hours, you have to be shut up inside a closed area, often with little ventilation or light, which can be stressful. Some tourists think a hurricane will be 'fun' and want to remain on island to see the storm. This is not a good idea. If you do remain you should register with your local consulate or embassy and email home as soon as the warning is given to alert your family that communications may go down and that you will follow the rules of the emergency services. You should be prepared to be inconvenienced and to help out in the clearing up afterwards. Team work in the aftermath of a disaster can be tremendous.

One of the best internet sites for information and data during an actual hurricane is www.stormcarib.com. The website of the **Hurricane Hunters** (www.hurricanehunters.com) has a virtual reality flight into the eye of a hurricane.

What to do

from cricket, golf and polo to diving and sailing

Canyoning

Dominica is one of the best places for canyoning in the Caribbean, if not the best. Created when volcanoes explode and cover the land with dust, which the rain then gradually erodes and washes away, canyons are very beautiful, with arches and spectacular architecture. Dominica has hundreds of rivers, some say 365 – one for every day of the year – and where there are canyons the water is a deep green with lovely reflections. Frequent and heavy rainfall in the forested mountains means that there is always plenty of water in the rivers. Experienced canyoners can explore on their own or go night canyoning (very dark), but should take advice first from Richard Metawi of **Extreme Dominica** (see page 111). The company offers an exciting adventure deep in the rainforest. A variety of locations are used, with hooks and bolts already drilled into the rock, including hot waterfalls, rappelling down waterfalls on to beaches and even negotiating Trafalgar Falls. The Titou Gorge has lots of water in the upper section, seven waterfalls in the middle section, the largest being around 65 ft, while the lowest section has the biggest drop. All levels of expertise are catered for.

Cricket

Since the Beausejour Cricket Ground was built in 2002, St Lucia has hosted a number of Test and international matches, including the World Cup in 2007. Women's cricket is strong in St Lucia and several St Lucian women play in the West Indies team. In 2004 left-hander Nadine George became the 1st West Indies woman to hit a century in a Test Match, scoring 118 against Pakistan in Karachi. Nicknamed 'The Lion', she was awarded an MBE in 2005. St Lucian men were not so prominent until Darren Sammy, from Micoud, was picked for the West Indies tour of England in 2007. Going from strength to strength, Sammy became the first ever St Lucian captain of the West Indies in 2010. In the highlight of his career, he guided his team to victory in the 2012 World Twenty20 in Sri Lanka.

In Dominica, cricket is among the most popular national sports. There is a women's league as well as men's. Two Dominican women have played for the West Indies women's team while five men have played for the men's team. Matches are played in some beautiful settings including at the national stadium called Windsor Park, the Botanical Gardens, and the Petite Savanne where two sides of the boundary line run along a cliff overlooking the Atlantic. See page 112.

Cycling

There are dedicated trails through the forest on **Anse Mamin Plantation** just north and part of the Anse Chastanet Estate (see page 74) in the southwest and on the **Errard Plantation** on the east coast of St Lucia. **St Lucia Cycling Association**, see Facebook, organizes road races, time trials and public fun rides. Cycling races are held on Independence Day starting at Castries market, with BMX, mountain bikes and road bikes and competitors of all ages.

There are lots of trails for off-road cycling in Dominica but, as yet, mountain biking is very small scale. Most people who cycle on the island bring their own bikes with them. Contact the **Dominica Cycling Association** (see Facebook) for more information. See also Getting around, page 134.

Diving

St Lucia

There is some very good diving off the west coast off St Lucia, although this is somewhat dependent on the weather, as heavy rain tends to create high sediment loads in the rivers and sea. Diving off the east coast is not so good and can be risky unless you are a competent diver. One of the best beach entry dives in the Caribbean is directly off **Anse Chastanet**, where an underwater shelf drops off from about 3 m down to 20 m and there is a good dive over **Turtle Reef** in the bay, where there are over 25 different types of coral. Below the **Petit Piton** are impressive sponge and coral communities on a drop to 70 m of spectacular wall. There are gorgonians, black coral trees, huge barrel sponges and plenty of other beautiful reef life. The area in front of the **Anse Chastanet Hotel** is a buoyed-off Marine Reserve, stretching from the west point at **Grand Caille North** to **Chamin Cove**. Only the hotel boats and local fishermen's canoes are allowed in. By the jetty, a roped-off area is used by snorkellers and beginner divers. Other popular dive sites include **Anse L'Ivrogne**, **Anse La Raye Point** (good snorkelling also at **Anse La Raye**) and the **Pinnacles** (an impressive site where four pinnacles rise to within 3 m of the surface), not forgetting the **wrecks**, such as the *Volga* (in 6 m of water north of Castries harbour, well broken up, subject to swell, requires caution), the *Waiwinette* (several miles south of Vieux Fort, strong currents, competent divers only), and the 55-m *Lesleen M* (deliberately sunk in 1986 off Anse Cochon Bay in 20 m of water). For dive operators, see page 74. Also see box, page 53.

Dominica

Dominica is highly regarded as a diving destination and has been featured in most diving magazines as 'undiscovered'. Features include wall dives, drop-offs, reefs, hot, freshwater springs under the sea, sponges, black coral, pinnacles and wrecks, all in unpolluted water. Due to steep drops the sediment falls away and visibility is excellent, at up to 30 m depending on the weather. Many drop-offs are close to the beaches but access is poor and boats are essential. There is a marine park conservation area in **Toucari Bay** and part of **Douglas Bay**, north of the Cabrits, but the most popular scuba sites are south of Roseau, at **Pointe Guignard**, **Soufrière Bay** and **Scotts Head**. An unusual site is **Champagne**, with underwater hot springs where you swim through bubbles, good for snorkelling. This area in the southeast, **Soufrière-Scotts Head**, is now a marine park without moorings so that all diving is drift diving and boats pick up divers where they surface. Along the south and southeast coast there are more dive sites but because of the Atlantic currents, these are for experienced, adventurous divers only. Note that the taking of conch, coral, lobster, sponge, turtle eggs, etc, is forbidden and you may not put down anchor in coral and on reefs; use the designated moorings. Snorkelling is good in the same general areas as diving, including **Douglas Bay** and the **Soufrière-Scotts Head Marine Reserve**. For dive operators, see page 113.

Fishing

On St Lucia, fishing trips for barracuda, mackerel, king fish, tuna, marlin, wahoo and other varieties can be arranged. Several sport fishing boats sail from **Rodney Bay** marina. There is an annual three-day billfish tournament in September. For more information, check www.worldwidefishing.com/stlucia.

On Dominica, fishing trips can be arranged with the captains of the whale-watching boats, see page 113.

Hiking and birdwatching

St Lucia

St Lucia has an extensive network of trails maintained by the Forestry Department, for which you need a permit (see page 75). In the north of the island is the **Forestière Rainforest Trail**, a 4.8-km/3-mile, two-hour walk along part of an old road from Castries to Gros Islet. **La Sorcière** and **Piton Flore** are densely forested mountains in the north with excellent rainforest vegetation. Piton Flore can be walked up in 40 minutes although it is a strenuous climb and you will need to ask how to get to the top, from where there are spectacular views. It is the last recorded location of Semper's warbler. There is a good chance of seeing the St Lucian parrot on the **Barre de l'Isle Rainforest Walk**. The **Des Cartiers Rainforest Trail** starts 9.5 km/6 miles west of Mahaut on the east coast and is a loop of about 4 km/2.5 miles taking around two hours through thick rainforest perfect for birdwatching, with many of the endemics found here. On the west coast is access to the **Millet Bird Sanctuary Trail** (closed at the time of writing), which meanders around the lake and the catchment area of the Roseau Dam through secondary rainforest, and is particularly good for birdwatching. In the **Edmund Forest Reserve** is the **Enbas Saut Trail** (below the falls), moderate to strenuous, at the foot of Mt Gimie, with a combination of rainforest, cloud forest and elfin woodlands. The 4-km/2.5-mile trail with 2112 steps has been cut down to the Troumassée River, where there are a couple of waterfalls and a pool where you can bathe. The **Edmund Rainforest Trail** runs through the forested heart of the island and, with prior arrangement, you can hike all the way across, joining up with the **Des Cartiers Rainforest Trail** in the east. See page 46.

Dominica

Hiking on Dominica can take anything from a couple of hours to a couple of weeks and there are plenty of guides and tour companies to show you the way to some outstanding sights and beauty spots. To visit any of the places maintained by the **Forestry, Wildlife and Parks Division** you will need a site pass, see box, page 92. The **Morne Trois Pitons National Park** contains trails to a number of natural wonders, such as the **Boiling Lake**, a strenuous hike of three hours uphill to the boiling fumarole, often taking in a stop at the **Valley of Desolation** along the way followed by a plunge into the waters of **Titou Gorge** to cool off. Other trails include the **Kent Gilbert Trail** and the **Middleham Trails**, from which you can see some of the many waterfalls on the island, or you can hike up **Morne Anglais**, one of the easier peaks to climb. Anyone wanting some serious hiking to get to know the island in depth should consider all or parts of the **Waitukubuli National Trail**, which covers the whole island, starting in the south, offering great opportunities for birdwatching as well as spotting other wildlife. See box, page 112. Remember that on either island, hiking in the forests can be wet and muddy, so bring appropriate clothing and footwear as well as hat, sun protection and insect repellent.

Sailing

St Lucia

As some of the best views are from the sea, it is recommended to take at least one boat trip. One of the most popular excursions is to sail down the west coast of St Lucia to **Soufrière**, where you stop to visit the volcano and some local sights, followed by lunch and return sail with a stop somewhere for swimming and snorkelling. Boats can also be hired with or without crew and charters can be arranged to sail to neighbouring islands. **Rodney Bay** is teeming with yachts in December for the **Atlantic Rally for Cruisers** race. See page 76.

Dominica
Dominica is not a major yacht charter centre and there is no marina, but yachts are available for hire and visiting yachts can anchor and get water and provisions. The three ports of entry are Portsmouth and Anse-de-Mai in the north and Roseau in the south, while the most popular anchorages are **Prince Rupert Bay**, **Mero**, and **Castle Comfort**. Both the **Anchorage Hotel** and **Fort Young Hotel** have docks for visiting craft. Excursions such as whale watching, diving and snorkelling trips and fishing usually incorporate elements of sightseeing and hospitality along the lines of day cruises offered on other islands.

Whale watching
Whale and dolphin watching is good off both islands, November-June is best, when sperm whales and humpbacks are seen.

St Lucia
20 different species of whales and dolphins have been seen in St Lucian waters, some of which are resident and some migratory, so whale watching takes place year round. The most commonly spotted whales are the pilot, sperm, humpback and false orcas, although orcas (killer whales) have also been seen on their way south. Dolphins include spinner, spotted, Fraser and bottlenose, usually in pods of 30-60 family members, but sometimes they can be seen hundreds at a time together. You can also look out for hawksbill and green turtles.

Dominica
Whale watching off Dominica is extremely popular, and the success rate is the best in the eastern Caribbean. The female whales and their calves are in the Caribbean waters for much of the year, with only the mature males leaving to feed for any length of time. If your trip is successful, you could be treated to the sight of mothers and their young swimming close to the boat, or young males making enormous jumps before diving below the waves. Dolphin are abundant too, particularly in the **Soufrière Bay** area and even if you miss the whales your boat is often accompanied by a school of playful dolphin. Several different types of whales have been spotted not far from the west shore where the deep, calm waters are ideal for these mammals. Sperm whales are regularly seen, especially during the winter months, as are

ON THE ROAD

Shopping in St Lucia and Dominica

Castries market is essential to visit to see all the fruit, vegetables, spices, arts, crafts, clothing and other souvenirs that St Lucia has to offer. All your senses will be bathed in the colour, smells, tastes and noise of the place. If you are self-catering, this is a good place to buy your fruit and veg, but the supermarkets are well stocked so you won't need to come here frequently. Look out for roadside stands, which are good places to pick up bananas or local delicacies. If you are in a self-catering cottage anywhere on Dominica, local farmers may visit with their fresh produce for sale. To buy fresh fish listen for the fishermen blowing their conch shells in the street; there is no fish shop in Roseau but fish can be bought at the **Fisheries Complex** or in the market on Friday and Saturday, get there early. Fishing villages such as Calibishie, Anse de Mai (north coast), Marigot (east coast) or Fond St Jean (south coast) are good sources of fresh fish; go down to the bay side around 1630 when the boats come in and get some kingfish or snapper for your evening meal.

There is a well-developed arts and crafts industry on St Lucia and several highly respected local artists sell their work as well as many ex-pat artists who have chosen to base themselves here. On either island, it is best to bring all your reading needs with you as bookshops are not well stocked. Islanders will appreciate any books you have finished with or you can donate them to a book swap.

large numbers of spinner and spotted dolphins. You can also sometimes see pilot whales, pseudorcas, pygmy sperm whales, bottlenose dolphins, Risso's dolphins and melon-headed whales. See page 114.

Windsurfing and kiteboarding

The winds off **Anse de Sables** in the southeast of St Lucia are very good for both windsurfing and kiteboarding, with the latter taking place off a cove slightly to the north. January, February, May and June are the best months with lots of wind blowing unobstructed cross-onshore from the left. The sickle-shaped beach is bordered leeward by **Moule à Chique Peninsula**, so you are safe from drifting off into the Atlantic. In the summer the wind is unreliable and the operators close until end-October. Windsurfing and kiteboarding is also good at **Cas-en-Bas** in the northeast, where the winds come in off the Atlantic. On the Caribbean side of the island several hotels offer equipment and **Reduit Beach** in Rodney Bay is good for beginners.

Where to stay

from all-inclusives to basic guesthouses

St Lucia

St Lucia has a wide and varied selection of hotels, guesthouses, apartments and villas. The majority of hotels are small, friendly and offer flexible service. They cater for all budgets, from the height of luxury to simple guesthouses in Gros Islet where you fall into bed after the Friday night jump-up. Most of the larger hotels are all-inclusive. Rodney Bay is the place to stay if you want the beach, restaurants and nightlife on your doorstep, while the marina makes excursions convenient by boat, whether for day sails, diving or whale watching. The northwest has the best beaches of golden sand and hotels here are convenient for golf and cricket, but still within striking distance of the action. Several hotels around Soufrière enjoy fabulous views of the Pitons and the coast, perched on hillsides in beautiful tropical gardens and forests; truly peaceful and romantic, but you would have to arrange car hire or taxis to get around or go to restaurants. Elsewhere, many of the hotels are remote resorts, providing everything their guests need for a relaxing holiday or honeymoon. Castries is obviously good for business travellers, but there is a beach and it is convenient for people who want to explore the island by bus. A good-value guesthouse will probably include breakfast, which may be anything from a slice of fruit and a bread roll to a full cooked spread of eggs and bacon or saltfish, allowing you to snack at lunchtime and afford a slap-up dinner in the evening.

Dominica

As a result of not being able to receive long-distance flights bringing mass tourism to the island, and not having any large beaches to put them on, Dominica has no large, all-inclusive resorts. Instead there are many small and intimate places to stay, whether high end or low budget or somewhere in between. There are hotels, guesthouses, bed and breakfast places, homestays and rental apartments, specialist dive lodges and rustic eco-resorts, inland or on the coast. You can camp, sleep in a tree house or a beach cottage (some named after members of the crew and cast of Pirates of the Caribbean who stayed there), opt for a luxury hotel room on the east coast where you can't swim but you can watch turtles, stay in a guesthouse in the Carib Territory overlooking the Atlantic, or at any number of small inns surrounded by bountiful gardens and the sounds of the forest. Some places may be a little rough around the edges, but if the paint is peeling it is more likely to be because of the ravages of the tropical climate and frequent rain rather than any lack of care by the owners.

Price codes

Where to stay

$$$$ over US$150

$$$ US$66-150

$$ US$30-65

$ under US$30

Price of a double room in high season, including taxes.

Restaurants

$$$ over US$12

$$ US$7-12

$ US$6 and under

Prices for a two-course meal for one person, excluding drinks or service charge.

Taxes Hotels in St Lucia add a 10-15% service charge and 8% VAT to the bill. Hotels in Dominica add 10% service and 10% VAT to the bill. Sometimes it is included in the rate, so it is worth checking. 15% VAT is added to meal charges and service charge may also be added.

Food
& drink

from Créole cooking to Nutz&Rum

Food

As you might expect of islands, there is a wide variety of seafood on offer which is fresh and tasty and served in a multitude of ways. Fish and seafood of all sorts are commonly available and are usually better quality than local meat. Beef and lamb are often imported from the USA or Argentina, but goat, pork and chicken are produced locally. There is no dairy industry to speak of, so cheeses are also usually imported. There is, however, a riot of tropical fruit and vegetables and a visit to a local market will give you the opportunity to see unusual and often unidentifiable objects as well as more familiar items found in supermarkets in Europe and North America but with 10 times the flavour.

The best bananas in the world are grown in the Windward Islands on small farms either organically or, at least, using the minimum of chemicals. They are cheap and incredibly sweet and unlike anything you can buy at home. You will come across many of the wonderful tropical fruits in the form of juices or ice-cream. Don't miss the rich flavours of the soursop (*chirimoya*, *guanábana*), the guava, tamarind or the sapodilla (*zapote*). Breakfast buffets are usually groaning under the weight of tropical fruits, from the bananas, pineapples, melons, oranges and grapefruit to mango, of which there are nearly 100 varieties, papaya/pawpaw (*papay* in Kwéyòl), carambola (star fruit) and sugar apple (custard apple or sweetsop). Mangoes in season drip off the trees and those that don't end up on your breakfast plate can be found squashed in abundance all over the roads. Caribbean oranges are often green when ripe, as there is no cold season to bring out the orange colour, and are meant for juicing not peeling. Portugals are like tangerines and easy to peel.

Avocados are nearly always sold unripe, so wait several days before attempting to eat them. Avocado trees provide a surplus of fruit so you will be doing everyone a favour if you eat as many as possible. Avocados have been around since the days of the Arawaks, who also cultivated cassava and cocoa, but many vegetables have their origins in the slave trade, brought over to provide a starchy diet for the slaves. The breadfruit, a common staple, rich in carbohydrates and vitamins A, B and C, was brought from the South Seas in 1793 by Captain Bligh, perhaps more famous for the mutiny on the *Bounty*. A large, round, starchy fruit, usually eaten fried or boiled, it grows on huge trees with enormous leaves and is known as *bwapen* in Kwéyòl. Christophene is another local vegetable which can be prepared in many ways, but is delicious baked in a cheese sauce. Dasheen is a root vegetable with green leaves, rather like spinach, which are used to make the tasty and nutritious callaloo soup. Plantains are eaten boiled or fried as a savoury vegetable, while green bananas, known as figs, can be cooked before they are ripe enough to eat raw as a fruit.

Cuisine

The style of cooking is known as Créole and is a mixture of all the cultural influences of the islands' immigrants over the centuries, from starchy vegetables to sustain African slaves to gourmet sauces and garnishes dating from the days when the French governed the islands. The movement of people along the chain of Caribbean islands means that you can also find rotis (pancake-like parcel of curried chicken and veg) from Trinidad and jerk meats from Jamaica, although these have been adapted from what you can expect on those islands. Fish and seafood are fresh and delicious, but make sure you only eat lobster and conch in season (September to April) to avoid overfishing. A local speciality is *accra*, a deep fried fish cake made of salted cod, an ingredient also used in saltfish and green fig, where the fig is actually green banana. *Bakes* are a fried dough patty filled with tuna, codfish or corned beef and the most popular snacks available in most bakeries. The term *provisions* on a menu refers to root vegetables: dasheen, yams, sweet potatoes, tannia, pumpkins, etc. In Dominica, you can try crab backs or *titiri* (fritters made with tiny fish). *Mountain chicken* (crapaud, or frog) used to be widely eaten, but is now critically endangered and should not be eaten, see box, above).

The small booklet, *Ti Gourmet Martinique*, gives many restaurants in Fort-de-France, with details and prices. Sampling the French and Créole cuisine is one of the great pleasures of visiting Martinique. A delightful blend of French, African, and Indian influences is found in Créole dishes, the cuisine is quite distinctive. These local specialities are not to be missed: *Ti-boudin*, a well-seasoned sausage; *blaff* is red snapper or other fish, possibly sea urchins (*chadrons*) cooked with local spices and onions, somewhere between a soup and a stew; *ragout*, a spicy stew often made with squid (*chatrous*), or conch

ON THE ROAD

Mountain chicken

Mountain chicken used to be the traditional national dish of Dominica. In reality it is not chicken, but a frog (*Leptodactylus fallax*) that tastes like chicken. It is currently found only in Dominica and Montserrat, although at one time it may have lived in at least seven islands. However, in both islands it is critically endangered, not just from over-hunting, introduced predators and habitat loss, but because of a pathogenic chytrid fungal skin condition, *Batrachochytrium dendrobatidis*, which caused the population on Dominica to plummet by 90%. One of the largest frog species in the world, its cultural importance to Dominica is such that it is found on the island's coat of arms.

Conservationists are working hard to save the species. Seven unaffected frogs were taken from Montserrat and Dominica to ZSL London Zoo, where they are part of a captive breeding programme. The female lays her eggs in a foam-filled burrow and when the tadpoles hatch, she feeds them with infertile eggs which she lays every few days especially for the purpose. It is hoped that frogs bred at the zoo in a bio-secure, temperature-controlled environment will be released into the wild when the danger of fungal disease has receded. So far, trial releases have been carried out with frogs radio-tracked and monitored by teams of field researchers. It is hoped that by monitoring disease distribution and prevalence and testing samples, researchers may discover how the mountain frog can survive, making it a case study which could be applied to the global amphibian crisis.

(*lambis*), or with meat; *colombo*, a recipe introduced by Hindu immigrants in the 19th century, is a thick curry; *poulet au coco*, chicken prepared with coconut; chunks of steakfish seasoned and grilled; *morue* (salt cod) made into sauces and *accras* (hot fishy fritters from Africa) or *chiquetaille* (grilled), or used in *feroce d'avocat*, a pulp of avocados, peppers and manioc flour; *langouste* (lobster), *crabe* (crab), *écrevisses*, *ouassous*, *z'habitants* (crayfish), *gambas* (prawns) and *vivaneau* (snapper) are often fricasseed, grilled or barbecued with hot pepper sauce. A good starter is *crabe farci* (stuffed land crab). Main dishes are usually accompanied by white rice, breadfruit, yams or *patate douce* (sweet potatoes) with plantains and red beans or lentils. *Christophine* (*Créole*: chayotte) *au gratin*; a large knobbly vegetable grilled with grated cheese and breadcrumbs, or fresh *crudités* are delicious, lighter side dishes. Fresh fruit often ends the meal; pineapples, papayas, soursops and bananas can be found all year round and mangoes, guavas and sugar apples in season. Ice cream (*glace*) is also a favourite dessert, particularly guava or soursop (corossol).

Drink

For non-alcoholic drinks, there is a range of refreshing fruit juices, including orange, mango, pineapple, grapefruit, lime, guava and passionfruit. Sorrel is also very popular. Coconut water sold by vendors is always refreshingly cool and sterile. Coconuts are picked unripe when they are full of water. Other local soft drinks include tamarind, a bitter sweet drink made from the pods of the tamarind tree. Teas are made from a variety of herbs, often for medicinal purposes. Cocoa tea, however, is drunk at breakfast as is hot chocolate, usually flavoured with spices. Try the sea-moss drink in Dominica, rather like a vanilla milk shake (with a reputation as an aphrodisiac), also drunk on Grenada.

Like most islands, St Lucia has its own rum, produced by **St Lucia Distillers**, used in cocktails and liqueurs or drunk on the rocks. There are over 20 different products, of which the amber Bounty is the most popular. Others include the white Crystal, used in cocktails, or the aged rums, Chairman's Reserve and Admiral's. Denros is a 150° proof rum to be treated with extreme caution. Rum shops stock five-gallon plastic containers of the stuff, combining it with fruits and spices and calling it 'spice'. Flavoured rums are popular with those who like an alcoholic, liquid sweet, including the award-winning Nutz&Rum. On Dominica you can find the local Macoucherie, Soca or Red Cap rums.

The local St Lucian beer is Piton, brewed in Vieux Fort. A shandy on St Lucia is a mixture of beer and ginger ale; if it's a Piton shandy it can be with lemon or sorrel. Kubuli is the local beer on Dominica. Both are drunk very cold for maximum refreshment.

Eating out

The standard of cooking in St Lucian restaurants is high, but for really authentic Créole food you should try local cafeterias and street vendors. Look out for home-made cassava bread and a local delicacy called *permi* made of cornmeal and coconut wrapped up in a banana leaf. A typical lunch at any of the stalls outside Castries market will include meat, plantains, potatoes, macaroni, rice and lettuce, washed down with a passionfruit juice.

The best places for freshly caught seafood on St Lucia, cooked to your specification, are the street parties at Anse La Raye, Dennery and Vieux Fort, where local fishermen sell their catch to be cooked on huge oil drum barbecues. You can get a snack at any time of day at a beach bar but most places open for breakfast from 0800-1000, lunch from 1200-1400 and dinner from 1800-2200. Hotels often start breakfast earlier, particularly if they are catering for an active crowd, such as divers, who need to be on the boat by

Coconut self-sufficiency

The ubiquitous coconut (*Cocos nucifera*) palm can be seen growing throughout the Caribbean and nuts often wash up on the eastern seaboard having been swept across the Atlantic from Africa. Although more people are killed worldwide by falling coconuts than by shark attacks, it is a miracle plant from top to bottom. The nutritious and thirst-quenching water of green coconuts is apparently considered sterile enough to give intravenously to a child dying of dehydration by inserting the needle into the coconut eye. You can also use it as an eye wash and it is effective against bladder infection. For a sore throat, a gargle of coconut water and crushed bird pepper (*Capsicum frutescens*) is recommended. The milk of a mature coconut is used in cooking, as is the fresh or desiccated flesh of the coconut. Leaves are plaited and lit to roast cashew nuts, or their ribs used to make yard brooms. The shell and husk are used to make copra for cooking oil and soaps and the husks are also used to stuff mattresses or light fires. Farmers use the husks to improve moisture retention in the soil and rotting roots make good compost. The remains of the shells can be made into charcoal. In construction, the trunk can be used as house pillars, while the leaves make good roofs and walls for kitchens and shelters. A cleaned coconut with seeds inside becomes a musical instrument, while children sometimes use them as a money box. Even the root has its uses, including treating impotency in men if an inch of it is steeped in rum. How much rum?

0900. Breakfast is usually swerved buffet style with croissants, pastries and fruit. Some restaurants will stay open late if they have a bar attached or there is live entertainment, but the kitchen usually closes by 2300.

Dominicans eat their main meal at lunch. On weekdays in the capital the lunch hour begins at 1300 and places fill up quickly. There are lots of 'snackettes' in Roseau and Portsmouth. If you are economizing, find a local place and choose the daily special, which will give you a chance to try the typical food.

St Lucia

Very popular as both a family holiday destination
and a romantic paradise for honeymooners, St Lucia
(pronounced 'Loosha') offers something for everyone.
Its beaches are golden or black sand, some with the
spectacular setting of the Pitons as a backdrop, and
many are favoured by turtles as a nesting site. Offshore
there is good diving and snorkelling, with a marine
park along part of the west coast. Rodney Bay is one
of the best marinas in the West Indies and windsurfing
and other watersports are available. The mountainous
interior is outstandingly beautiful and there are several
forest reserves to protect the St Lucian parrot and other
wildlife. Sightseeing opportunities include sulphur
springs, colonial fortifications and plantation tours.
St Lucia has a rich cultural heritage, having alternated
between the French and English colonial powers, both
of whom used African slaves, and has produced some
of the finest writers and artists in the region. The island
has the distinction of having produced two Nobel
prize winners, the highest per capita number of Nobel
Laureates ever, anywhere.

Best for
Empty beaches ■ Nightlife ■ Watersports

Castries

one of the Caribbean's busiest port cities; spreading from the seashore up steep hillsides

The picturesque capital, Castries, is set on a natural harbour against a mountainous background. Ships of all sizes come in here: mammoth cruise ships, cargo and container ships, the ferry to Dominica and the French Antilles, yachts and brightly painted fishing boats, all jostling for space at their respective berths. The centre of Castries is small enough to walk around, but to get to outlying districts you can catch a bus (minivan) or call a cab. There are lots of car hire companies if you want to drive yourself.

★ Market area and around

Largely rebuilt after being destroyed by four major fires, the last in 1948, the city's commercial centre and government offices are built of concrete. Only the buildings to the south of Derek Walcott Square and behind Brazil Street were saved. Here you will see late 19th- and early 20th-century French-style wooden

Essential St Lucia

Finding your feet

Hewanorra, the international airport, is in the south of the island, about two hours' drive from Castries and the beach resorts in the northwest. The smaller short-haul George F Charles Airport is on the Vigie Peninsula, just outside Castries, from where you can get a taxi or bus transfer to the capital. If you are arriving on the international ferry from Dominica, the terminal is on the south side of Castries' harbour, a short taxi ride from any of the hotels in and around the capital.

Getting around

Hiring a car is the best way of exploring the island, but remember that the mountain roads into the forests are very poor. A 4WD or high-clearance vehicle is recommended. If you don't want to drive yourself, there are tours to anywhere you might want to go and guides can always be arranged. The **Forestry Department** (page 75) and **Heritage Tours** (page 78) are well placed to organize customized itineraries. Minibuses provide a reasonable public transport system but will not get you far off the beaten track.

Weather Castries

January	February	March	April	May	June
29°C 22°C 95mm	29°C 22°C 69mm	30°C 22°C 60mm	30°C 23°C 74mm	31°C 24°C 88mm	31°C 25°C 131mm

July	August	September	October	November	December
31°C 24°C 171mm	31°C 24°C 219mm	32°C 24°C 200mm	31°C 23°C 250mm	30°C 23°C 222mm	30°C 22°C 138mm

St Lucia

Pointe du Cap
Smuggler's Cove
Cap Estate
Pointe Hardy
Pigeon Island Historic Park
Anse Lavoutte
Fort Rodney
Cas-en-Bas
10 **20** **32** Massade
Gros Islet
Comerette Point
Beausejour
Anse Comerette
Cricket Ground
Anse Lapins
Rodney Bay
14 Rodney Bay
Espérance Harbour
Labrellotte Bay
13 **21** Bois d'Orange
Monchy
Port Dauphin
Cap Marquis
8
Marisule Estate
Grande Rivière
Cassimi Point
Choc Bay
5
14
Marquis River
Morne Monier
Rat Island
Union Agricultural Station
Marquis Point
Vide Bouteille Point
Gablewoods Mall
Tanti Point
Vigie Beach
11 **31**
Paix Bouche
D'Estrées Point
1 **12**
Vigie
Grande Anse
La Toc Bay
Morne Chaubourg
La Toc Point
Castries
Babonneau
Desbarra
Coubaril Point
Morne Fortune
Tortue Point
Fort Charlotte
Fond Cacao
Fond Assor
Fond Latisab Creole Park
Goodlands
15
Chassin
Louvet Point
Cul de Sac Bay
Forestière
Rain Forest Adventures
Anse Massacré
Hess Oil Terminal
Castries Waterworks Forest Reserve
Anse Louvet
Marigot Bay
La Sorcière
Povert Pt
9 **23**
Piton Flore
Roseau Bay
6
St Lucia Distillery
La Croix Maingot
Au Leon
La Caye
Massacré
Jacmel
Vanard
Bexon
Ravine Poisson
Grande Rivière
Mamelles Pt
Fond d'Or Nature Reserve
& Historical Park
Fond D'Or Bay
Pointe La Ville
Anse La Raye
Sarot
Morne Beaujolais
Dennery
Dennery Bay
Anse Cochon
Plas Kassav
33
Morne La Combe
Errard
Treetop Adventure Park
Linnis Point
Anse Jambette
Canaries
Millet
Fregate Island Nature Reserve
Anse La Liberté
Grand Bois Forest
Praslin
Mamiku Gardens
3
Praslin Bay
Blanche Point
Mon Repos
Trou Gras Point
Anse Chapeau
17
Morne Tabac (2224 ft)
Anse Chastanet
24
Diamond Falls Botanical Gardens & Mineral Baths
Quillesse Forest Reserve
Mahaut
Patience
Grand Caille Point
30
Morne Gimie (3118 ft)
Port Volet
22
Soufrière
18
Soufrière Bay
Morne Coubaril Estate
19
Sulphur Springs
Edmond Forest Reserve
Latille Gardens
Fond Bay
Micoud
Petit Piton
Fond St Jacques
Rabot Estate
Fond Doux Estate
Ti Rocher
27 **4** **7** **2** **16**
Etangs
Morne Grand Magazin (2022 ft)
Blanchard
Troumassé Bay
Anse des Pitons
Tet Paul Nature Trail
Fond Gens Libre
Fond Doux Holiday Plantation
Desruisseaux
Gros Piton
Monzie
Belle Vue
Anse Ger
Anse l'Ivrogne
Victoria Jnct
Dacretin
Saltibus
Point Lamarre
Caraïbe Point
Industry
Banse
Pierrot
Anse L'Islet
Gertrine
Choiseul
Sauzay
Augier
Savannes Bay Nature Reserve
Balenbouche
2 Piaye
Laborie
26
Laborie Bay
Vieux Fort
25
Maria Islands Nature Reserve
Black Bay
28
Anse de Sables
Caesar Point
Cap Moule à Chique

N

2 km
2 miles

Best views on St Lucia

Castries from the Inniskilling
  Monument, page 38
Morne Gimie from Cap Moule à
  Chique lighthouse, page 48
Soufrière and the west coast from
  the top of Gros Piton, page 54
Praslin Bay from the Foxgrove Inn,
  page 61
The Pitons from Ladera Resort,
  page 62

Best empty beaches

Grand Anse, page 40
Anse Lavoutte, page 44
Anse de Sables, page 47
Maria Islands, page 47
Laborie, page 57

Best local eats

Castries central market vendors,
  page 35
Dennery fish fest on the beach at
  weekends, page 45
Anse La Raye fish fry on Fridays,
  page 49
Roots Bar, page 68
Martha's Tables, page 69

Fact file

Location One of the Windward Islands
chain lying between the Atlantic Ocean
and the Caribbean Sea, with Martinique
to the north and St Vincent to the south
Capital Castries, 14° 1' 0" N, 60° 59' 0" W
Time zone Atlantic standard time.
GMT -4hrs, EST +1hr
Telephone country code +758
Currency East Caribbean dollar, EC$

buildings with three storeys, their gingerbread fretwork balconies overhanging the pavement. The other area which survived was the 1894 iron market on the north side of Jeremie Street. A new market has been built next door to house the many fruit, vegetable and flower sellers on the ground floor, while on the first floor and in an arcade opposite are vendors of T-shirts, crafts, spices, basket work,

Castries

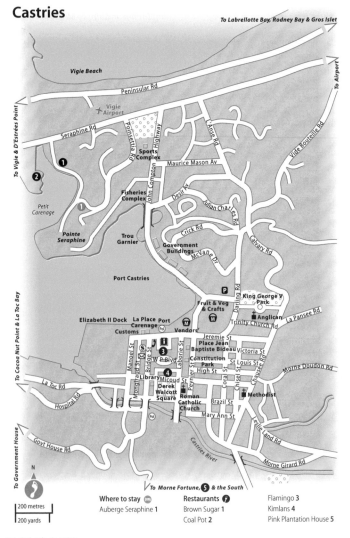

To Labrellotte Bay, Rodney Bay & Gros Islet

Vigie Beach

Peninsular Rd

To Airport

Vigie Airport

Seraphine Rd

To Vigie & D'Estrées Point

Poinsetta Rd

L'Anse Rd

John Compton Highway

Vide Bouteille Rd

Sports Complex

Maurice Mason Av

Fisheries Complex

Desir Av

Julian Charles Rd

Petit Carenage

Crick Rd

Calvary Rd

Pointe Seraphine

Trou Garnier

Government Buildings

McVane Dr

Port Castries

King George V Park

Darling Rd

Fruit & Veg & Crafts

Elizabeth II Dock

La Place Port Carenage

Anglican

Trinity Church Rd

La Pansee Rd

Customs

Vendors

Jeremie St

Place Jean Baptiste Bideau

Victoria St

To Cocoa Nut Point & La Toc Bay

Manoel St

Bridge St

SJP Blvd

Laborie St

Constitution Park

High St

St Louis St

Coral St

Chisel St

Chausse

Morne Doudon Rd

Library

Micoud St

Peynier St

Derek Walcott Square

Roman Catholic Church

Brazil St

Methodist

La Toc Rd

Hospital Rd

Mary Ann St

Leslie Land Rd

To Government House

Govt House Rd

Castries River

Morne Girard Rd

To Morne Fortune, **5** & the South

N

200 metres
200 yards

Where to stay	Restaurants	
Auberge Seraphine 1	Brown Sugar 1	Flamingo 3
	Coal Pot 2	Kimlans 4
		Pink Plantation House 5

BACKGROUND
Derek Walcott

One of the Caribbean's most renowned poets and playwrights in the English language, Derek Walcott, was born in St Lucia in 1930. He has published many collections of poems, an autobiography in verse, *Another Life*, critical works, and over 20 plays such as the prize-winning *Dream on Monkey Mountain* uses English poetic traditions, with a close understanding of the inner magic of the language (Robert Graves), to expose the historical and cultural facets of the Caribbean. His books are highly recommended, including his narrative poem *Omeros*, which contributed to his winning the 1992 Nobel Prize for Literature. He lived and worked for many years in Trinidad and later in the USA. Since 2010 he has been Professor of Poetry at the University of Essex in the UK and in 2011 he won the TS Eliot *Prize for White Egrets* (2010). He still spends much of his time in St Lucia.

leeches and hot pepper sauce. This is a wonderful place to stock up on a lifetime's supply of cinnamon sticks which, together with the cocoa sticks on offer, can be made into delicious hot chocolate, known as cocoa tea.

On the eastern side of the old market there is a little arcade with small booths where vendors provide good vegetarian food, Créole meals and local juices. In total, there are some 300 full time vendors but this swells to around 400 on Saturday, which is the traditional market day. If there are cruise ships in port that day, Castries is heaving with people. Vendors are inclined to give you the hard sell, but if you're not interested just give them a polite 'No thank you' and move on. On the other hand, if you are interested in buying, haggling over price is acceptable.

Hours can be spent wandering around the stalls taking in the sights, sounds and smells, listening to the vendors chatting in Kwéyòl, sampling some of the local food and deciding what souvenirs to take home or what fruit to snack on during your stay. There are duty-free shopping centres for cruise ship passengers at La Place Carenage by the main dock and at Pointe Seraphine to the north, reached by water taxi across the harbour or by road around the bay. The tallest building in the city is the seven-storey Financial Centre at the corner of Jeremie and Bridge Streets, with a joyous sculpture by local artist, Ricky George.

Derek Walcott Square

Derek Walcott Square was the site of the Place D'Armes in 1768 when the town transferred from Vigie. Renamed Promenade Square, it then became Columbus Square in 1893. In 1993 it was renamed in honour of poet Derek Walcott and contains busts of both Nobel Laureates. It was the original site of the courthouse and the market and is now used for ceremonial occasions and entertainment, including concerts during the Jazz Festival. The **library**, built by US millionaire Andrew Carnegie, is on its west side. The giant Saman tree in the middle is about 400 years old.

Brazil Street

Running along the south side of Derek Walcott Square, Brazil Street has several buildings which survived the fire of 1948 and are therefore some of the oldest in the capital. Here you can see latticed overhanging balconies and gingerbread fretwork. There are even some remaining chattel houses, made of wood on a stone base. They were built in such a way as to be easily dismantled if necessary; families often had to move with 'all their goods and chattels'.

Cathedral of the Immaculate Conception

On the east side of Derek Walcott Square is the Roman Catholic Cathedral of the Immaculate Conception which bursts into colour inside. Suffused with yellow light, the side altars are often covered with flowers while votive candles placed in red, green and yellow jars give a fairy tale effect. The ceiling, supported by iron arches and braces, is decorated with panelled portraits of the apostles. Above the central altar with its four carved screens, the apse ceiling has paintings of five female saints with St Lucy in the centre. The walls have murals by Dunstan St Omer, one of St Lucia's better known artists. They are of the stations of the cross and are unusual in that the people in the paintings are black. The 12 stained-glass windows were created by his son, Giovanni.

Folk Research Centre

Mount Pleasant, T758-452 2279, www.stluciafolk.org, Mon-Fri 0830-1630.

The Folk Research Centre is an old manor house originally owned by the Devaux family and is a fine example of colonial architecture. The centre is dedicated to documenting the language and culture of St Lucia and has done much to preserve Kwéyòl and make it a written as well as a spoken language. There is a collection of musical instruments and an extensive multimedia library on folklore and history.

La Toc

On the southern tip of the bay is **La Toc Point**, where a **battery** ⓘ *T758-452 6039, daily 0900-1500*, was built as part of the fortifications to protect the harbour. This is the best restored military fort of the 60 forts around Castries, visited mostly by cruise ship visitors. There are cannon on the thick walls, underground rooms and corridors with exhibits of artefacts found in and around the area, including a collection of over 900 bottles found by divers in Castries harbour. It was completed in 1888 to repel a potential attack from the USA when Castries was still a valuable coaling harbour. However, as the threat disappeared, the fort was abandoned from 1905 until it was bought in 1982 by Alice Bagshaw.

At **Bagshaw's Studio** ⓘ *T758-452 7921, Mon-Fri 0830-1600, Sat 0830-1200*, you can buy attractive silkscreen clothes and household linens and visit the print shop to watch the screen printing process. The company is very highly regarded and was commissioned to make prints for Queen Elizabeth II and outfits for her grandsons, Princes William and Harry, when they were little. Carry your return air ticket for a discount.

Morne Fortuné

The ridge of Morne Fortuné just south of the city centre enjoys wonderful views over Castries and the harbour and receives pleasant breezes to temper the tropical sunshine. For this reason the British built their grand houses up here as well as their military buildings. From the town centre, head south down Micoud Street then turn right into Government House Road, up the hill and onto Morne Road. It is very twisty and steep and dangerous to walk because of traffic negotiating the bends.

Government House with its curious metalwork crown can be seen from the road and dates from 1895. The house is not open to the public but there is a small museum with a collection of photos artefacts and documents, called **Le Pavillon Royal Museum** ⓘ *T758-452 2481, Tue and Thu 1000-1200, 1400-1600, by appointment only, donations welcome*. **Caribelle Batik** ⓘ *T758-452 3785, www. caribellebatikstlucia.com, Mon-Fri 0800-1600, Sat-Sun 0800-1200, Sun if a cruise ship is in port*, is just past Government House on Old Victoria Road. Its home in the pretty Howelton House with its typical Victorian architecture is worth a visit and it affords a lovely view over the capital. You can see the batik studio and print shop, see how the fabric is printed on sea-island cotton and then made into vibrant clothes and furnishings full of tropical colour.

In the hills behind the military complex (see below) is **Eudovic's Art Studio** ⓘ *T758-452 2747, www.eudovicart.com, Mon-Fri 0730-1630, Sat-Sun 0730-1500*, where woodcarvers produce abstract artwork from local hardwoods. Eudovic and his artistic family also run a guesthouse and restaurant.

Military sites on Morne Fortuné There are six historical military sites on Morne Fortuné under the control of the **National Trust of St Lucia** ⓘ *www.slunatrust. org*, which runs tours of the area. They were built for obvious strategic reasons as you can see most of the northwest coast and the town from the top of the 260-m hill. The fortifications were started by the French in 1768, but expanded and completed by the British. Most of the buildings and the ruins are used for housing or educational purposes.

Fort Charlotte, the old Morne Fortuné fortress, is now the Sir Arthur Lewis Community College. The **Apostles' Battery** (1888-1890) was built by the British long after the threat from France had gone, but at a time when the port was important as a coaling station and the harbour needed protecting. It was built at ground level so you couldn't see it from the sea. There are four cannon, each weighing four tons.

The **Powder Magazine**, the **Guard Cells** and the stables next to them were constructed in 1763-1765 by the French and are probably the oldest buildings on the Morne. The walls of the Powder Magazine are thick enough to contain any accidental explosion from the gunpowder and ammunition stored there. **Provost's Redoubt** (1782) was a lookout point and from here you can see as far as Martinique on a clear day. Next to the lookout an open patch of grassland is planned as a National Heroes Park and Monument. The French and British **cemeteries** are beside each other in a residential area. Five British and one French

ON THE ROAD
The port of Castries, then and now

The first settlement and fortification built by the French in the 18th century was at Vigie, stretching along the coast to Choc Bay, and known as Petit Carénage. However, in 1768-1771 the main fort was moved up to Morne Fortune and the government buildings, including Government House, followed. The town then relocated to its present position and was eventually named Castries by the British, after the Maréchal de Castries a French governor in 1780, having briefly enjoyed the name of Felicité Ville during the French Revolution and the aftermath. In the second half of the 19th century Britain decided to develop the port of Castries for coal bunkering. Welsh coal was brought to St Lucia and sold on to passing steam ships, so that by the turn of the century Castries was the 14th most important port in the world in terms of tonnage handled. However, by the 1930s oil had superseded coal and the port declined. During the Second World War two ships in the harbour were torpedoed by a German submarine. A third torpedo missed its target: an Alcoa ship carrying a full cargo of TNT which might have blown the whole of Castries to smithereens. In 1948 most of the town was engulfed in flames and many buildings destroyed when a fire started in a tailor's shop, although fortunately there was no loss of life. Further fires caused damage in 1951 and 1963, when about a third of the town was burned down. Castries officially became a city in 1967. Nowadays, buoyed by tourism, the port is again thriving, receiving some of the largest craft in the world: cruise ships.

governor are buried here, as well as military personnel and civilians, many of whom died of malaria and yellow fever.

The most spectacular view is from the **Inniskilling Monument** at the far side of the college (just beyond the old Combermere barracks) where you get a fine view of the town, coast, mountains and Martinique. It was here in 1796 that General Moore launched an attack on the French who, together with the Brigands had gained control of the island after defeating the British at Vieux Fort and Rabot. The steep slopes give some idea of how fierce the two days of fighting must have been. As a rare honour, the 27th Inniskilling Fusiliers were allowed to fly their regimental flag for one hour after they took the fortress before the Union Jack was raised. The monument was built at the eastern end of Fort Charlotte in 1932 to commemorate the event. Sir Arthur Lewis, Nobel Laureate in Economics, is buried in front of the monument.

Vigie

Castries harbour is protected on three sides by hills, of which the **Vigie Peninsula** is the northern promontory. The word Vigie comes from the French term for having someone posted as lookout and both the French and the English saw its strategic advantage and built defensive military positions there, making the entire peninsula a military stronghold. The **Vigie Lighthouse** was built in 1914, although a lookout of sorts was used as far back as 1768. Its light can be seen 30 miles out to sea and the 36-foot tower overlooks 18th- and 19th-century barracks, military ruins and other historic buildings. **Vigie Beach** is a lovely strip of sand with plenty of shade, popular and cleaned regularly. Its only drawback is that it runs parallel with the airport runway, but that is compensated by the lack of hotels (except at one end). The airport is used for inter-island flights with small aircraft, so they don't take long to take off or land and the noise soon passes.

North of Castries
the island's tranquil interior with good hiking and an Atlantic turtle-nesting beach

The part of the island to the north of Castries is the principal resort area; it contains the best beaches and the hotels are largely self-contained. It is also the driest part of the island. Inland are a number of interesting places to visit.

Union Agricultural Station
The John Compton highway leaves Castries past Vigie and follows the curves of Vigie Beach and Choc Bay. Where the road leaves the bay and just before it crosses the Choc River, a right turn to Babonneau will take you past the Union Agricultural Station (about one mile), the site of the **Forestry Department Headquarters** ⓘ *T758-468 5649, www.forestryeeunit.blogspot.co.uk*. There is a visitor centre, nature trail and a small, well-run **Union Zoo**, where you can see indigenous species such as the agouti and the endemic St Lucia parrot as well as iguanas. The Forestry Department organizes hiking across the island.

Babonneau and Fond Assau
Continuing inland you come to rural villages in St Lucia's heartland, most of them unaffected by tourism. **Babonneau** and **Fond Assau** are villages where it is believed the last group of African slaves were brought, as there are still strong African traditions. At Fond Assau is the **Fond Latisab Créole Park** ⓘ *T758-450 5461, Sun-Fri, tours by appointment*, a 10-acre working farm producing honey, cocoa and spices, such as nutmeg and cinnamon. Visitors are given demonstrations of traditional methods of agriculture and other skills. Drumming is still used as a means of communication, while wood cutting is done with a two-man saw accompanied by drums, singing and a *chak chak* band. Crayfishing is done using bamboo pots and you can see how they make *farine*, or flour, from cassava before making it into bread.

Rain Forest Adventures
Chassin, T758-458 5151, www.rainforestadventure.com, closed Mon, Fri-Sat, online prices US$45-95, depending on activity, hotel transfers available, booking essential.

Further along the road, **Rain Forest Adventures** is a popular attraction, particularly with cruise ship visitors, where you are taken up the side of La Sorcière hill in a

gondola seating eight. You ascend at one level and descend at a higher level through the forest canopy, so you see two layers of rainforest, all of which is explained by the guides. There are great views of both sides of the island and across to Martinique in the distance. You can also **zipline** through the forest for an adrenaline rush, with the option to do it at 1800 when it gets dark, and hike the **Jacquot Trail** with a naturalist guide during the day or at 0600 to see birds (four to five hours). The guides are professional and fun, there is a good standard of safety and most people are fit enough to take part.

★Desbarra and Grand Anse

An alternative road from Babonneau leads east to **Desbarra** and the east coast at **Grand Anse**. This is a long, windy beach and one of the most important nesting sites in the Caribbean for the leatherback turtle (see box, page 42). Patrols of the beach monitor the turtles and try to protect them from human activity. The beach has been the target of illegal sand mining and the Grand Anse Estate is earmarked for a tourist resort. Much of the estate is currently abandoned, providing an invaluable habitat to wildlife, including iguanas, the fer-de-lance snake, the boa constrictor and rare birds. Visits to Grand Anse to see the turtles can only be done in organized groups and from March to August. The Desbarra community conducts overnight camping trips with trained guides, organized by **Heritage Tours** ① *T758-458 1454, www.heritagetoursstlucia.org.*

Rodney Bay

the place to come for an action-packed beach holiday and nightlife

This whole area supports a mass of tourist facilities – hotels, restaurants, shops and clubs – between the lovely beach at Reduit and the first-class Rodney Bay Marina, but it was formerly the site of the US Naval Air Station of Reduit. Built in 1941, the Americans made an attempt to reclaim the swamps and the bay was dredged. It was the first of a chain of bases established to protect the Panama Canal and supported a squadron of sea planes. Closed in 1947, it was not until the 1970s when a causeway to Pigeon Island and a marina were built that the wetlands vanished.

Rodney Bay is an excellent base for watersports, both on the beach and from the marina. Take the left turn off the main road at the junction leading to **Bay Walk Mall**, to reach the hotels and restaurants. At the end of the road there is good access to **Reduit Beach**.

Gros Islet

The normally sleepy fishing village of Gros Islet, just north of the marina, has a few guesthouses and cheap and cheerful bars along the beach and in the village. It is not a glitzy tourist destination, but it holds a popular **jump-up** in the street each Friday night, with music, dancing, bars and cheap food (more tourists than locals but enjoyed by night owls). Things start to get lively and loud from 2200-2300.

Inland from here, taking the turning opposite Elliot's Shell filling station by the fire station, you will come to the **Beausejour Cricket Ground**, St Lucia's flagship ground for international test matches and host, in 2007, to World Cricket Cup matches and in 2010 to the ICC World Twenty20 Championship.

Rodney Bay

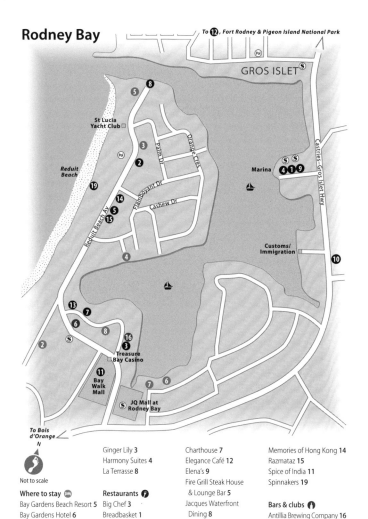

Where to stay

Bay Gardens Beach Resort 5
Bay Gardens Hotel 6
Bay Gardens Inn 7
Coco Palm 2

Restaurants

Big Chef 3
Breadbasket 1
Buzz 2
Café Olé 4
Ginger Lily 3
Harmony Suites 4
La Terrasse 8

Charthouse 7
Elegance Café 12
Elena's 9
Fire Grill Steak House
  & Lounge Bar 5
Jacques Waterfront
  Dining 8
Key Largo 10
Lime 13

Memories of Hong Kong 14
Razmataz 15
Spice of India 11
Spinnakers 19

Bars & clubs

Antillia Brewing Company 16
Delirius 6

Not to scale

ON THE ROAD

Turtles at Grand Anse

A massive turtle slips from the ocean waves and pauses on the edge of the surf. All is quiet. In the light of the moon, she hauls her heavy body further up the beach. A cluster of people stand motionless and nearly breathless, fearful that the giant sea turtle will sense them and return to the ocean without laying her eggs.

The leatherback turtle (*Demochelys coriacea*) roams the open oceans, feeding on a diet of jellyfish, including the deadly Portuguese Man-o-war, which is why the meat of the leatherback is not usually eaten as it can be toxic. Leatherback turtles here weigh around 800-1000 lbs, but male leatherbacks can reach a length of 2.5 m (8 ft) and weigh up to 2000 lbs. Only a mature female comes ashore and then only to make a nest and lay 60-120 eggs, perhaps several times in one season but only every two to three years. Leatherbacks require sandy nesting beaches backed with vegetation and sloped sufficiently so that the crawl to dry sand is not too far. A suitable depth of coarse, dry sand is important, because the female first excavates a pit for her body and then must reach moist sand before she can make the proper flask-shaped nest. Incubation takes from 55 to 74 days and emergence of the hatchlings occurs at night. The turtles are believed to reach maturity in six to 10 years and may live to the grand age of 80. Hawksbill and Green turtles also come ashore here but not so often.

All sea turtles are endangered. Sand mining or construction close to the water destroy habitats, while they also face human and other animal and bird predators. Their diet is one reason why they frequently fall prey to marine pollution, eating plastic bags because they look like jellyfish.

Pigeon Island
former military outpost covered in ruins to explore and the venue for festival concerts

About ¾ mile after Elliot's Shell filling station on the outskirts of Gros Islet, turn left to Pigeon Island National Landmark, once an island, now joined to the mainland by a causeway on which large hotels have been built. Access to the causeway's beach is being squeezed into an ever-smaller area.

Pigeon Island National Park
Daily 0900-1700, entry to park and museum US$7 visitors, EC$7 residents, children 5-12 EC$3, beach chair rental EC$5/US$2 (entry free after 1700 but only to the restaurants, see page 67).

The park, at the end of the causeway, was opened by Princess Alexandra on 23 February 1979 as part of St Lucia's Independence celebrations. It has two peaks which are joined by a saddle. The higher peak rises to about 360 ft. On the lower of the two peaks lies **Fort Rodney**. You can climb both of them, a steep, hot walk.

Managed by the National Trust, the island is of considerable archaeological and historical interest. Amerindian remains have been found, the French pirate François Leclerc (known as Jamb de Bois for his wooden leg) used the large cave on the north shore and the Duke of Montagu tried to colonize the island in 1722 (but abandoned it after one afternoon). From here, Admiral Rodney set sail in 1782 to meet the French navy at the Battle of Les Saintes. It was captured in 1795 by the Brigands (French slaves freed by the leaders of the French Revolution) but was retaken in 1798 by the English. Used as a quarantine centre from 1842 it was abandoned in 1904 but became a US observation post during the Second World War.

The island finally became the home of Josset Agnes Huchinson, a member of the D'Oyly Carte Theatre, who leased the island from 1937 to 1976. The bay became a busy yacht haven and 'Joss' held large parties to entertain the crews. Her abandoned house can still be seen on the south shore of the island. The small and poorly maintained **interpretation centre** is in the Officers' Mess and rebuilt to the original design. It shares the building with the offices of the St Lucia National Trust. There are two small beaches and a café on Pigeon Island, which you can get to by water taxi from Rodney Bay if you don't have a car.

North coast
wild and untamed rocky coastline and beaches, good for hiking and beachcombing

The road north passes through the Cap Estate with its luxury villas, hotels and golf course to Pointe du Cap. This is the driest part of the island, formerly sugar cane land now given over to housing and tourism. There is a hotel on nearly every beach, even some of those on the Atlantic side of the island. Tucked away on the extreme north coast in the heavily developed, 3000-acre Cap Estate, is the relatively new Morne Pavillon Nature Reserve, which covers 18 acres. Once part of the area where the French grew cotton at the beginning of the 18th century, by the early 20th century it belonged to the Floissac family. Much of the north was leased to the US military in 1942 to build a base to protect the island from German submarines, should they invade Martinique across the channel. By 1943, however, the threat had receded and the base was abandoned. The land then changed hands a couple of times until it was bought in 1966 by Herbert Lutz, who started to build but never completed a home on the site. His heirs donated the land to the St Lucia National Trust in 2010 after a local campaign to keep this small green space surrounded by the extensive residential development.

Cas-en-Bas Beach
A relatively safe Atlantic beach worth visiting is Cas-en-Bas, which is popular with kitesurfers and has a laid-back beach bar and restaurant. Unfortunately it is also used by horse riding tour parties, so the sand is not always clean, but you can pick your spot away from the activities. Note that although riding on the beach is a romantic notion for some, for the ponies it can be torture. They are worked very hard on rough tracks and sand, causing their feet to get sore. It is not uncommon

to find them lame on all four feet, while the combination of sweat and salt water causes sores under their tack. Many are also very thin, with worms and not enough to eat. The bay is shallow and protected by offshore reefs and usually very calm. Seaweed can occasionally be a problem.

Walks around Cas-en-Bas

A good circular walk from Gros Islet can be done to Cas-en-Bas taking the road past La Panache Guesthouse down to the beach, then following tracks north until you reach the golf course, from where you return along the west coast to Gros Islet.

Alternatively you can drive through the golf course to the Cotton Bay Villa Resort. The road ends at the resort, but you can continue on foot down a track to the sand. Another golf course is planned for this area, but in the meantime you will see cacti, wild scenery and Martinique.

To the south of Cas-en-Bas Beach are **Anse Lavoutte**, **Anse Comerette** and **Anse Lapins**. Follow the rocks, it is a 30-minute walk to the first and an hour to the last. They are deserted, windswept beaches and headlands.

East coast to Vieux Fort
dramatic Atlantic coast dotted with beaches and fishing villages

Barre le l'Isle

The transinsular road goes through extensive banana plantations before climbing steeply over the Barre de l'Isle, the mountain barrier that divides the island. There is a short, self-guided trail at the high point on the road between Castries and Dennery, which takes about 10 minutes and affords good views of the rainforest and down the Roseau Valley. There is a small picnic shelter. It can be slippery after rain. The experience is rather spoilt by the noise of traffic.

A longer walk to **Mount La Combe** ⓘ *guides available Mon-Fri 0830-1500, pay on site, US$10*, along the Barre de l'Isle ridge, can also be undertaken from this point, returning on the same trail. Allow an hour if you go to the foot of Mount La Combe and another hour if you hike the steep climb to the top, total two hours round trip. From the peak you get panoramic views of Roseau and Mabouya valleys. You may hear, even if you don't see, the St Lucia parrot on the trail, as well as many other birds such as the St Lucia oreole and St Lucia warbler. Park by a snack bar on the main road where the Forestry Department guides wait. Be careful in this area as it is known as the drug-growing region. Cyclists and hikers have reported that the locals are not particularly friendly and their stares can make you feel uncomfortable.

Fond d'Or Bay

The road descends with spectacular Atlantic views through Grande Rivière down the Mabouya Valley to Fond d'Or Bay and **Fond d'Or Nature Reserve and Historical Park** ⓘ *St Lucia Heritage Tours, www.heritagetoursstlucia.org, open daily*, a former estate with the remains of a sugar mill, windmill and the plantation house, which is now an interpretation centre. There is also an Amerindian site, mangrove and estuarine forest and trails through dry scrub woodland to a sandy beach (swimming is dangerous) where leatherback turtles come to nest.

The rocks at the head of the bay are known as the **Mabouya Man** and his sleeping lion because of their shapes. The name Mabouya comes from 'Ma Boyé' which means 'without beginning' and is closely associated with snakes (there are boa constrictors in the park). Mabouya was believed to be a mischievous spirit needing constant reverence to prevent him bringing misfortune on man. Children still fear the Mabouya, who figures in scary tales. The park is popular for picnics and is closely associated with the annual **Jazz Festival**, hosting some of the leading events.

Dennery

Dennery is set in a sheltered bay with **Dennery Island** guarding its entrance and dominated by the Roman Catholic church. Here you can see the distinctive St Lucia fishing boats pulled up on the beach. Carved out of single tree trunks, the bows are straight and pointed rather than curved and are all named with phrases such as *God help me*. At the weekend the town invites visitors to a **fish fest**, when from 1600 to 0200 you can join in a street party, eat freshly caught and cooked seafood and enjoy music and dancing. The main East Coast Road hugs the hillside, bypassing the town below. There is a bar/restaurant with a spectacular view over Dennery Bay, worth a stop for refreshment.

Treetop Adventure Park

T758-458 0908, http://adventuretourstlucia.com, Mon-Sat 0800-1600, although daily for cruise passengers, US$20 for children, US$59 for adult zipline if booked online, transfers available.

Inland from Dennery along the Dennery River, this adventure park has 12 ziplines (including the highest and longest on the island) where you are strapped into a harness and slide down a cable from one platform to another through the forest canopy. Plenty of instruction, excellent guides and time to look around you on the platforms up in the trees above the river. There's even a zipline adventure for children from the age of three. There are add-on activities on certain days of the week including jeep and hike to Errard Falls, where you can swim in the pool at the base of the waterfall, mountain biking or hiking through the forest to Dennery Waterfall for a cold dip in the pool. Errard Plantation is often included on tours of the east coast, where you can see nutmeg and cocoa grown and processed as well as visit the falls.

Praslin Bay and around

Just after Dennery you will see **Praslin Island** in Praslin Bay, one of only three islands where St Lucian whiptails live. This endemic lizard (*Cnemidophorus vanzoi*) had its population decimated by introduced cats, rats and mongooses and used to live only on Maria Major Island until being successfully introduced here in the

1990s to prevent extinction and then in 2008 to Rat Island off Castries. A fourth colony on Dennery Island is planned. The only whiptail found in the eastern Caribbean, the males patriotically wear the colours of the St Lucian flag: black, white, blue and yellow. The village of Praslin is a fishing community known for its traditional boat building.

Fregate Islands Nature Reserve ⓘ *National Trust, on the north side of Praslin Bay, T758-452 5005, natrust@candw.lc, closed to the public.* The reserve has two small islands, nesting sites for the frigate bird, Fregata magnificens, which migrates from Cape Verde. Birds nest on the offshore rocks although their numbers have seriously declined. The dry forest also harbours the trembler, the St Lucian oriole and the ramier. The reserve includes a section of mangrove and is the natural habitat of the boa constrictor. On land you will see the abandoned construction site of a huge resort which was supposed to have a golf course and marina.

Mamiku Gardens ⓘ *between Praslin and Mon Repos, T758-455 3729, see Facebook, daily 0900-1700, EC$20 for foreigners, EC$10 for locals.* The botanical gardens and woodland walks on an estate once owned by Baron de Micoud when he was governor of the island for France in the 18th century but later a British military post. There is an ongoing excavation at Mamiku which is producing interesting finds from the ruins of the house where the British soldiers were surprised and massacred by the Brigands. The gardens are lovely and full of birds; you can take a guided tour or wander around among the frangipani and ginger lilies with a map and plant guide. There are several different sections, including a bush medicine garden, but every plant is numbered for easy identification. There is also a snack bar and souvenir shop, or picnic tables if you want to take your own food.

Micoud

The East Coast Road continues south, regaining the coast at Micoud, known for its wine: banana, guava, pineapple, ginger and sugar cane varieties, brewed and bottled under Helen Brand. One mile west of Micoud is **Latille Gardens** *(www. heritagetoursstlucia.org)*, with organic fruit, flowers, herbs, trees and waterfall which cascades into a deep pool where you can swim.

Des Cartiers Rainforest Trail

Forestry Dept, T758-715 0350/450 2231 for reservations, www.malff.com, Mon-Fri 0830-1500, US$10 includes guide; other times by prior negotiation will cost more.

Six miles west of Mahaut, signed from the road, is the start of this trail. It follows through a figure of eight loop and is about 4 km/2.5 miles taking about two hours, starting from the rangers' station, where there are toilets. The path is clear and level, but there are lots of steps which can be slippery and you have to watch where you're putting your feet. The rainforest here is thick and lush and it is perfect for birdwatching, with many of the endemics found here. Ask about arranging early morning visits for parrot spotting. You can also arrange a longer, more strenuous six- to seven-hour hike through the Quilesse Forest and Edmund Forest Reserves to Fond St Jacques, just outside Soufrière on the west coast.

Savannes Bay

Red and black mangrove swamps can be seen at **Savannes Bay Nature Reserve**. at **Mankoté Mangrove** to the south and on **Scorpion Island** in the bay. The shallow waters of Savannes Bay are protected by a reef, making it an ideal breeding ground for conch and sea eggs as well as the cultivation of sea moss, grown on ropes suspended just below the surface of the sea by hundreds of plastic bottles as buoys. There are archaeological sites on **Saltibus Point** and **Pointe de Caille**. Boats going to the Maria Islands will often deviate to take you there if you ask, or you can book a kayak tour or rent a boat from Anse de Sables.

Anse de Sables Beach

The road continues south until it reaches the international airport. The perimeter road skirts Anse de Sables Beach, the longest stretch of golden sand beach on the island. You can walk for miles along adjoining beaches and hardly see a soul, despite the presence of a resort to the north. On the main part of the beach you can find a beach bar, basic accommodation, windsurfing and kitesurfing. January and February are the best months for wind but May is also good. From mid-June to the end of October the winds are unreliable because of the hurricane season and the schools may be closed.

★Maria Islands

T758-454 5014, www.slunatrust.org, entry by prior reservation only, preferably a few days in advance as they have to find a boat and captain, US$28/EC$75 per person minimum 4 people, or pay for 4 and go alone, for boat and guide; package of transport, tour, lunch available; able swimmers only.

Across from Anse de Sables Beach, just offshore, these National Trust islands are home to two endemic reptiles: a colourful lizard and small, rare, harmless snake, the Kouwès or couresse snake. The lizard (*Cnemidophorus vanzoi*) is known as *zandoli te* in Kwéyòl. The males, about 18 cm long, sport the colours of the national flag. The females are brown with some white spots along their belly. The snake likes to keep damp and cool and can often be found in the hollow of a forked tree where a pool of water has collected.

There's a pleasant, small beach on Maria Major and excellent snorkelling, which makes a good full-day trip. Tour operators will provide snorkelling gear but the National Trust does not, so take your own. Unauthorized access (including windsurfers from Anse de Sables) to the islands is not allowed. From May to August public access is restricted or prohibited while migrating seabirds are nesting in their hundreds on the cliffs and on the ground.

Vieux Fort
St Lucia's second, and most southerly city, host to the international airport and industrial zone

Vieux Fort is the island's industrial centre, with a Free Zone and the Hewanorra International Airport. It is an active town with a good Saturday market, supermarkets, cinema and a lot of traditional housing. The police station and post office, on Theodore Street, are right in the middle of the town. The bus terminal is at the end of Clarke Street near the airport.

There is evidence that the Amerindians had many settlements in the southern part of the island and cultivated crops on the relatively flat land in the foothills of the central mountains. Archaeologists have found remains of houses and petroglyphs all around the southern coast. It is believed that the Dutch were the first Europeans to try and settle in the south around 1600, but later it became an important sugar cane area with both the French and British using imported slave labour on the plantations. In the Second World War, the Americans built an airbase here which has now become the island's main airport. Their presence brought prosperity, giving local people and immigrants from other islands jobs and a market for their produce. Rum shops, night clubs and dance halls flourished, as did typhoid, tuberculosis and venereal disease, but the US military drained most of the swamps and eradicated malaria. The era was known as *an tan Laméwichains* (at the time of the Americans), but after the base was dismantled in 1949 the economy declined.

Cap Moule à Chique
Cap Moule à Chique is the most southerly point on the island, with a **lighthouse**, from where you can see the Pitons, Morne Gomier (1028 ft) with Morne Grand Magazin (2022 ft) behind it. Unfortunately Morne Gimie (3118 ft) is largely obscured. Further to the east is Piton St Esprit (1919 ft) and Morne Durocher (1055 ft) near Praslin. The lighthouse itself is 730 ft above sea level and also has good views over the Maria islands and southwest to St Vincent.

West coast to Soufrière
an area of outstanding beauty and biodiversity

The West Coast Road is in excellent condition with good signposting. It is a curvy, but spectacular, drive down to Soufrière. Stunning mountain scenery and dozens of pretty bays make this the most beautiful part of the island.

Marigot Bay
On reaching the Roseau Valley, take the signposted road to Marigot Bay, a beautiful inlet and natural harbour which provided the setting for the 1967 film, *Dr Doolittle*. It supports a large marina and, not surprisingly, a large number of yachts in transit berth here to restock with supplies. There is a police station and immigration post, bars, disco, restaurants and accommodation. A small strip of land juts out into the bay and has a little beach, reached by water taxi. The **Marigot Bay Marine Reserve**

supports the largest mangrove system on the west coast and includes fringing reefs to both the north and south entrance to the bay.

Roseau Valley

The Roseau Valley is the principal banana-growing area on the island and everywhere you look there are bananas. The valley is prone to mudslides and flooding during storms, which periodically wipe out the whole crop. It used to be a big sugar-growing area and for that reason there is a rum distillery here. **St Lucia Distillers** ① *T758-456 3148, www.saintluciarums.com, Mon-Fri 0900-1500, reservations mandatory, call 24 hrs in advance, US$10,* have excellent tours of the factory, contrasting old and modern methods of rum production and you can taste over 20 different flavours and buy their produce, see Drink, page 26. There is also a 19th-century steam-powered sugar mill with a narrow-gauge railway and steam engine used to carry sugar cane and molasses.

Millet Bird Sanctuary Trail

Closed at the time of writing; check with the Forestry Department. 45 mins from Castries. Turn left opposite the turning to the rum distillery and then right at Vanard; or by going to Anse la Raye and turning left as you get through the village on the road past La Sikwi. The Forestry station is at the end of the road after the village of Millet. Forestry Department, T451 1691, sluforestrails@hotmail.com, Mon-Fri 0830-1500, US$10, weekends by prior arrangement with higher prices, birdwatching tours by reservation 24 hrs in advance, US$30, starting early in the morning and lasting over 4 hrs, bus route 3B from Castries to Millet.

This area of secondary rainforest in the heart of the island at 1000 ft above sea level is one of the best places for birdwatching. The land has been acquired by the Forestry Department to protect the Roseau Dam on the property and its watershed, with farmers being given land elsewhere. There is a high biodiversity with many fruit trees as well as forest and over 30 species of bird can be found here, including five endemics: the St Lucia parrot, St Lucia black finch, St Lucia oriole, St Lucia pewee and St Lucia warbler. The well-maintained, 1.75-mile loop trail takes about two hours to walk with only one steep section up to a panoramic view of **Morne Gimie**, the forest and Roseau Dam, the largest stretch of water in the Eastern Caribbean. If you want to see parrots it is best to arrange a tour at dawn, but you can see birds at any time of day.

Anse La Raye and around

The main road continues to Soufrière and passes through the fishing villages of Anse La Raye and **Canaries** (no facilities), where you can see old wooden cottages, many of them with attractive decorative details and verandas. Anse La Raye has become very popular for its fish fry on the seafront road on Fridays, which attracts hundreds of people to eat lobster in season and fish and seafood at any time of year, freshly caught and cooked on coal pots and barbecues at stalls along the street. Tables are laid out in the road and it is a good opportunity to try local accompaniments such as breadfruit salad, floats and bakes. During the day the street is lined with souvenir stalls but it is worth visiting the bakery on the road just before you get to the seafront. They still use a traditional oven and produce delicious hot turnovers, a sweet bread roll stuffed with coconut and sugar.

More local delicacies can be sampled on the road heading south; just before Canaries on one of the curves, where the road widens, is **Plas Kassav** ① *T758-459 4050, daily 0830-1900.* Here, a family bakery makes farine (cassava flour) to produce delicious cassava bread in many flavours, both sweet and savoury: salt, saltfish, smoked herring, peanut butter, cinnamon, coconut, chocolate, cherry and raisin. On the way to Soufrière, a favourite stop with St Lucians and tourists alike, the shop also sells hot pepper sauces, honey and other local products.

Soufrière
picturesque town flanked by the majestic Pitons; a major tourist draw

After Canaries the road goes inland and skirts Mount Tabac (2224 ft) before descending into Soufrière. This is the most picturesque and interesting town on the island, with marvellous old wooden buildings at the foot of the spectacular Pitons, now a UNESCO World Heritage Site. The town does, however, have a reputation for hassling; tour parties are usually whisked through to avoid unwanted attention.

Soufrière dates back to 1713 when Louis XIV of France granted the lands around Soufrière to the Devaux family. The estate subsequently produced cotton, tobacco, coffee and cocoa. During the French Revolution, the guillotine was raised in the square by the Brigands but the Devaux family were protected by loyal slaves and escaped.

There are lots of French **colonial houses** with shutters and overhanging balconies with gingerbread fretwork, creating shady walkways around the square. Unfortunately many of them are crumbling and haven't had the attention and investment that the old houses around Derek Walcott Square in Castries have received. A **market** lies to the north of the harbour, where you can buy straw hats, crafts, spices and coal pots, but the **waterfront** is the centre of action, particularly on Saturdays when a fruit and vegetable market is held here and in the streets off it. The water here is extremely deep and reaches 200 ft only a few yards from the shore, which is why boats moor close in.

There is a dark sand beach to the north of the bay in front of the **Hummingbird Beach Resort** and lots of colourful wooden fishing boats pulled up on the shore. A conch shell is blown when fish has been landed.

Diamond Falls Botanical Gardens and Mineral Baths
T758-459 7155, www.diamondstlucia.com, Mon-Sat 1000-1700, Sun and holidays 1000-1500, EC$17.50/US$7, children half price, EC$15/US$6 to use the public outdoor hot baths, EC$17.50/US$7 for private bath; only official guides are allowed in, do not accept offers from those at the gates; all the car parks are free, no matter what some people may tell you.

From the square in Soufrière, take Sir Arthur Lewis Street east past the church and look for a right hand turning to reach the botanical gardens and mineral baths. An old mill and waterwheel on the property date back to 1765 when the estate grew sugar cane. Later, after the decline of sugar, it went into lime oil production and the old vats can still be seen. British sailors on board ships travelling between the West Indies and Europe used to drink a daily spoonful of vitamin C-rich lime oil to combat scurvy and for that reason became known as 'Limeys'.

The baths were developed in 1784 after Baron de Laborie sent samples taken from sulphur springs near the Diamond River to Paris for analysis. They found minerals present which were equivalent to those found in the spa town of Aix-la-Chapelle and were said to be effective against rheumatism and other complaints. The French king ordered baths to be built. Despite being destroyed in the French Revolution, they were eventually rebuilt and can be used by the public. The gardens date back to 1983. Planted by Mrs Joan Devaux, they are better than ever; well maintained and many native plants can be seen.

Anse Chastanet and beaches near Soufrière

Good swimming, snorkelling and diving is offered from the beach and in the marine park at Anse Chastanet. It is best to take a water taxi from Soufrière, as the one-mile track at the north end of the beach (past the yacht club) is very rough and taxis sometimes refuse to go down there.

This is one of the best beach entry dives in the Caribbean and an absolute must if you enjoy snorkelling (the south end near the jetty is superb but keep within the roped-off area; the north end is also good with some rocks to explore, but avoid the middle where boats come in). Day sail boats often stop here for snorkelling and a swim in the afternoon on their return to Castries. The hotel has a good and inexpensive restaurant (although if you are on a budget you may prefer to take a picnic) and the dive shop is extremely helpful, they will hire out equipment by the hour. The beach is public.

The Sourfrière Marine Management Association preserves the environment between **Anse Jambon**, north of **Anse Chastanet**, and **Anse L'Ivrogne** to the south. They have placed moorings in the reserve, which yachts are required to use, with charges based on the size of the boat. Divers also have a marine park fee included in the cost of a dive.

South of Soufrière

rainforest-covered volcanoes and some of the island's top natural attractions

Morne Coubaril Estate and around

Opposite the turning to Sugar Beach (formerly Jalousie Plantation Resort) on the Vieux Fort road, T758-459 7340/712 5808, www.stluciaziplining.com, daily 0900-1600, estate tour US$11, ziplining US$76.

Another former Devaux plantation, Morne Coubaril Estate was bought in 1960 by Donald Monplaisir and is a working farm of 113 ha (280 acres), producing cocoa, coffee, copra, coconuts, orange, grapefruit, lime, bananas and any number of tropical fruits. A short tour of the estate does not include the plantation house, in which the Monplaisir family still lives, but you can see it from the outside, as well as a replica workers' village. Popular with tour parties, the estate now includes ziplining with a view of the Pitons and the town of Soufrière.

On the other side of the road from Morne Coubaril Estate, in the valley between Petit Piton and Gros Piton, a luxury resort, **Sugar Beach/Jalousie Plantation Resort and Spa**, was built despite complaints from ecological groups and evidence from archaeologists that it is located on a major Amerindian site. An important burial ground is believed to be under the tennis courts and there have been many finds of petroglyphs and pottery.

Halfway along the drive to **Jalousie** you will see a little sign to a small, warm waterfall on your left. Someone will collect a fee for access. Relax in the warm waters. There are also petroglyphs on the **Stonefield Estate** which are believed to date from AD 350 and can be found along the Estate's nature trail through the forest. This used to be a cocoa plantation but is now providing luxury villa accommodation with a spectacular view of the Pitons and a restaurant.

Sulphur Springs

T758-459 5726, www.soufrierefoundation.org, daily 0900-1700, EC$20/US$8, compulsory tour with guide takes about 30 mins; EC$12.50/US$5 bath or EC$27.5/US$11 combination ticket; buses to Vieux Fort pass the entrance, from where it is a 5- to 10-min walk.

These springs are the big attraction in the area, and you will be able to smell them before you reach them. Originally a huge volcano about 3 miles in diameter, it collapsed some 40,000 years ago leaving the west part of the rim empty (where you drive in). The sign welcomes you to the world's only drive-in volcano, although actually you have to stop at a car park. These sulphur springs are the only one still active, although there are seven cones within the old crater as well as the Pitons which are thought to be volcanic plugs. Tradition has it that the Arawak deity **Yokahu** slept here and it was therefore the site of human sacrifices. The Caribs were less superstitious but still named it *Qualibou*, the place of death. Water is heated to 180°F and in some springs to 275°F. It quickly cools to about 87°F below the bridge at the entrance. From the main viewing platform, you can see over a moonscape of bubbling, mineral rich, grey mud. There are two pools you can bathe in: Black Water Pool is the hotter, at 38.7°C, while the smaller Pool of Love reaches 31.3°C. There are also souvenir stalls, an interpretation and a trail.

Rabot Estate

The turning for the Sulphur Springs is by the entrance for the Rabot Estate, a recently rehabilitated 56-ha/140-acre cocoa plantation now owned by the British chocolatier, Hotel Chocolat. Dating back to 1745, and the oldest cocoa plantation on the island, it contains some very rare old trees. The cocoa grown here and bought from local farmers is made in the UK into their St Lucia chocolate bar, but

IN THE WATER

Coral reef

A diving or snorkelling trip over a tropical reef allows a first-hand experience of this habitat's diversity of wildlife. There are a number of good field guides to reef fish and animals; some are even printed on waterproof paper. Among the commonest fish are the grunts, butterfly, soldier, squirrel and angel fish. Tiny damsel fish are very territorial and may even attempt to nip swimmers who venture too close to their territories (more surprising than painful).

There are over 50 species of hard coral (the form that builds reefs) with a variety of sizes and colours. Among the most dramatic are the stagshorn and elkhorn corals, which are found on the more exposed outer reefs. Brain coral forms massive round structures up to 2 m high and pillar coral forms columns that may also reach 2 m in height. Soft corals, which include black corals, sea fans and gorgonians, colonize the surface of the hard coral adding colour and variety. Associated with these structures is a host of animals and plants. Spiny lobsters may be seen lurking in holes and crevices along with other crustaceans and reef fish. The patches of sand between outcrops of coral provide suitable habitat for conch and other shellfish. The islands now restrict the collection and sale of corals (especially black corals) and there are legal restrictions on the sale of black corals under CITES. Overfishing has also affected conch and lobster in places.

The delights of swimming on a coral reef need to be tempered by a few words of caution. Many people assume the water will be seething with sharks, however these animals are fairly uncommon in nearshore waters and the species most likely to be encountered is the nurse shark, which is harmless unless provoked. Other fish to keep an eye open for include the scorpion fish with its poisonous dorsal spines; it frequently lies stationary on coral reefs. Moray eels may be encountered, a fearsome looking fish, but harmless unless provoked at which point they can inflict serious bites. Of far more concern should be the variety of stinging invertebrates that are found on coral reefs. The most obvious is fire coral, which comes in a range of shapes and sizes but is recognizable by the white tips to its branches. In addition, many corals have sharp edges and branches that can graze and cut. Another common group of stinging invertebrates are the fire worms, which have white bristles. As with the fire coral, these can inflict a painful sting if handled or brushed against. Large black sea urchins are also common on some reefs and their spines can penetrate unprotected skin very easily. The best advice when observing coral reefs and their wildlife is to look and not touch.

a factory is being built on the island so that the whole bean-to-bar process can be done here. A modern, luxury hotel, spa and restaurant have been built here for total immersion in all things chocolate.

Fond Doux Estate

T758-459 7545, www.fonddouxestate.com, daily 0800-1600 for tours, until 2200 for dinner.

This estate, just south of Rabot in the hills, was one of the first established by the French in the 18th century. First growing cocoa and coffee, then sugar, it is still producing cocoa while embracing tourism. There are charming cottages where you can stay and the estate is open for tour groups who receive a tour showing traditional methods of drying and grinding cocoa beans and how cocoa grows, identifying flowers and fruit trees and sampling various fruits. The 1864 plantation house is a typical single-storey wooden construction with a veranda and outside kitchen, surrounded by pleasant gardens. The owners still live in the house but doors and windows are left open for visitors to look in.

Tet Paul Nature Trail

Chateau Belair, T758-459 7200, daily 0900-1700, EC$12.5/US$5 for adult foreigners, EC$5/US$2 for children.

Opposite the entrance to Fond Doux is this community tourism project. The easy to moderate trail is guided and you are shown traditional farming and cooking methods as well as medicinal plants, fruit trees and birds. The highlight of the 45-minute trail, however, is the scenery, with spectacular views of the Pitons, Jalousie Bay, Morne Gimie and the whole of the southern part of the island to Vieux Fort and as far as Maria Island.

★The Pitons

Petit Piton (2437 ft) is a volcanic plug rising sheer out of the sea and since June 2004 a UNESCO World Heritage Site, along with its sister, **Gros Piton** (2526 ft). It is a focal point of all views around Soufrière. It is possible to climb Petit Piton, an extremely steep ascent, but it is not encouraged. Local guides will take you up, but it is dangerous and you will be damaging the mountain. South of Soufrière, near Union Vale estate, is the **Gros Piton Trail** ⓘ *Fond Gens Libre, Gros Piton Tour Guide Association, T758-459 9748, grospitontours@candw.lc, see also http://soufrierefoundation.org/gros-piton-nature-trail, guides can be found at the Interpretative Centre, 0700-1400, price depends on the party and who you are, start early, wear good boots.*

The village of **Fond Gens Libre** is at the base of the mountain, accessible by jeep or high-clearance car although you will have to ford a couple of streams. The trip up and back is about four hours through the different ecosystems of the mountain, with stops to look at brigand caves and tunnels. It is strenuous, so you must be in good physical condition. It should not be attempted in wet weather even though the trail has been improved.

★Enbas Saut and Edmund Forest trails

Six miles east of Soufrière through Fond St Jacques (where the church contains paintings by Dunstan St Omer) and up a poor road is the rangers' station for the

Forest birds

St Lucia oriole (carouge) (*Icterus laudabilis*) Measuring 20-22 cm, mostly black with orange patches on the upper wing-coverts, under wing-coverts, rump, abdomen, flanks and under tail-coverts.

Blue-hooded euphonia (perruche; jacquot carim) (*Euphonia musica*) 12 cm long with a yellow forehead and blue head while the body is mostly green above and yellowish green underneath.

St Lucia warbler (sikwi barbade; petit chit) Formerly Adelaide's warbler (*Dendroica adelaidae*) but reclassified because it has black round the eyes, not white. The upper parts are grey and the underparts bright yellow.

Purple-throated carib (kilibri rouge) (*Eulampis jugularis*) A sturdy 13-cm hummingbird with dark plumage and purplish red throat but noticeable for its metallic green wings.

Semper's warbler (pied blanc) (*Leucopeza semperi*) Last seen in 2003 but not confirmed and classified as critically endangered, it has dark grey upper parts and whitish underparts and measures 14.5 cm.

St Lucia parrot (jacquot) (*Amazona versicolor*) Now around 800 parrots in the wild, up from 100 a few years ago. They are mostly green with a bluish head, a touch of maroon on the underparts, red on the foreneck and a red patch on the wing.

St Lucia black finch (moisson; pyé blan) (*Melanospiza richardsoni*) 13-14 cm, the male is black with pink feet, the female is greyer.

Trembler (twanblè) (*Cinclocerthia ruficauda*) A dark brown to olive-grey bird measuring 23-25 cm with greyish-white underparts and a long, slender bill. It really does tremble.

Rufous-throated solitaire (siffleur montagne) (*Myadestes genibarbis*) Mostly grey, about 19 cm, with a rufous throat, foreneck and posterior underparts.

Pearly-eyed thrasher (gwo grieve) (*Margarops fuscatus*) Rather like a thrush, the 28-cm thrasher has a heavy brownish yellow bill, its upper parts are dark greyish-brown and its underparts are white with greyish-brown markings.

St Lucia pewee (pin caca) Formerly lesser Antillean pewee (*Contopus latirostris*) but reclassified because of colour differences. A flycatcher about 17 cm with rufous coloured underparts and olive-grey upper parts.

Enbas Saut Trail ⓘ *Forestry Dept, T758-468 5649, sluforestrails@hotmail.com, daily 0830-1500, US$10 with or without a guide.* In dense rainforest in the Central Forest Reserve, there is a good chance of seeing a variety of woodland birds. You will hear the St Lucia parrot even if you are not lucky enough to see it. The vegetation is a mix of rainforest, cloud forest and elfin woodland, with glorious views of the three peaks of Piton Canarie, Piton Troumassee and Mount Gimie. The 4-km/2.5-mile trail has been cut down to the Troumassee River, where there are a couple of waterfalls and a pool where you can bathe. It is a moderate to strenuous hike as there are 2112 steps down and back up again and the hillside is steep, not recommended for those with breathing difficulties or heart problems. You can also expect to get wet and muddy and good footwear is essential. There are a couple of river crossings to negotiate. At the falls there are picnic tables and a screen behind which you can change your clothes for swimming. There are toilets at the Rangers' station at the start of the trail.

From the rangers' station you can instead continue along the track to hike the **Edmund Forest Trail**. With prior arrangement you can hike with a guide through the Edmund Forest Reserve and the Quilesse Forest Reserve to the east side and down to the Des Cartiers Rainforest Trail.

The southwest
less mountainous and more agricultural with fishing villages and historical interest

There is abundant evidence that before the arrival of Europeans, the fertile soils of the interior were farmed and pottery has been found scattered over large areas in Saltibus and Parc Estate in the southwest. When the Amerindians were too far from the coast to live on fish, they ate iguanas, crabs, crawfish and other animals.

The best known archaeological site on St Lucia is at **Pointe de Caille**, which has been investigated many times by teams of archaeologists, including one from the University of Vienna in the 1980s. The site has evidence of all the peoples that have lived on St Lucia (with the possible exception of the Caribs). The shells and bones of the animals they ate are there, as well as pottery and tools.

The road around the southwest to Vieux Fort is in good condition. Along the way you pass **Choiseul**, a small town with ruined fortifications and petroglyphs in the area. It is known for its handicrafts, promoted by **La Fargue Craft Centre**, on the main road, where local artisans sell clay pots, baskets, woodcarvings, spices and sauces. Other artisans have stalls along the road or you can ask to see the work of local artists in their homes. There used to be more craftspeople here, but when the road was still poor, many relocated to areas with better communications.

Balenbouche Estate
T758-444 1244, www.balenbouche.com.

Southeast along the coast, this former sugar plantation, now reduced to 30 ha/75 acres, consists of a beautiful 19th-century **Great House** set in gardens with magnificent old trees, and the ruins of a sugar mill, including an historic aqueduct. Rustic cottages are dotted around the grounds and the property is used as a yoga retreat, for weddings, or just a quiet holiday.

There are Arawak **petroglyphs** on rocks in the Balenbouche River. If you wade along the river and look up, you will see faces staring down at you from the top of the ravine, the work of the Amerindians who used to live on the terraces above the deep ravine. Evidence of their farming tools have been found there, including red flakes of jasper (red flint) and stone artifacts such as axes, adzes and hammers, used instead of metal tools. You will probably need somebody to show you the way from Balenbouche Estate or Saltibus.

Laborie

The last town before reaching Vieux Fort, Laborie is by-passed by the new road but worth a detour. It is a small fishing community set in a lovely bay with a good beach, the best in the area. The centre of the town has many wooden colonial buildings; there are a few guesthouses and some good, local restaurants. The place comes alive on Friday nights when there activities, shows and music.

Tourist information

There are tourist information centres at George F Charles airport and in the duty-free shopping centres at Pointe Seraphine and Place Carenage where the cruise ships come in.

Tip...

The website **www.stlucianow.com** has lots of useful and up-to-date information.

Where to stay

Castries *p31, map p34*

$$$$ Rendezvous
Malabar Beach, T758-457 7900,
www.theromanticholiday.com.
Medium-sized, pretty, all-inclusive hotel for couples at the end of Vigie Beach beyond the cemetery, very romantic, specializes in weddings and honeymoons. Good value in that all sports, even scuba diving, are included, food is good and drinks are branded. Service is excellent, friendly and attentive.

$$$ Auberge Seraphine
Vigie Marina, T758-453 2073,
www.aubergeseraphine.com.
A gleaming white, modern hotel on the edge of the harbour close to Vigie airport. 22 rooms on 2 levels, terrace and pool with good views of the boats. Attractive and well run, very pleasantly located. Flocks of egrets fly in to roost here in the trees by the lily pond. Good restaurant.

$$$ Casa del Vega
South side of Vigie Peninsula,
T758-459 0780, www.casadelvega.com.
Rooms and studios, also 3- to 5-bedroom apartments, kitchen facilities, on a little cove on Clarke Av overlooking the harbour, 96 steps down to little beach, watersports, spa treatments, restaurant, about a mile to Vigie Beach and the airport. Helpful owners, nothing is too much trouble.

$$ Eudovic's Guest House
Goodlands, T758-452 2747,
eudovic@candw.lc.
On the same premises as Eudovic's Studio, see page 37, 10 mins from city centre. The family of woodcarvers and artists run this simple, friendly guesthouse and have made all the furniture from local wood.

North of Castries *p39, map p32*

$$$$ Calabash Cove
Bonaire Estate, Marisule, T758-456 3500,
www.calabashcove.com.
Very attractive beachfront property on a small cove, intimate and relaxing, excellent service and food. All hillside rooms and beachfront cottages have sea view, lovely for sunset watching. All-inclusive option.

$$$$ East Winds
Labrelotte Bay, T758-452 8212,
www.eastwinds.com.
Set in gorgeous gardens covering 12 acres, this small and elegant all-inclusive hotel has 30 rooms, most of which are in pretty pastel-coloured bungalows in traditional style. There are lovely views of the bay and beach

and gourmet food, romantic dining, piano bar and afternoon tea.

$$$$ Villa Beach Cottages
Choc Beach, T758-450 2884, www.villabeachcottages.com.
Under same ownership as **La Dauphine Estate**. Beachfront villa suites sandwiched between the main road and the sea next to **The Wharf** restaurant, with gingerbread fretwork, wooden shutters and jalousies, 1 or 2 bedrooms with 4-poster beds, kitchen, living room, balcony with hammocks, Derek Walcott used to spend his holidays here before it became so glamorous.

$$$$-$$$ Windjammer Landing
Labrellotte Bay, T758-452 0913, www.windjammer-landing.com.
A lovely hillside setting but isolated, 30-min walk to a bus route. Villa complex with hotel facilities, 1-bedroom suites, 2- to 4-bedroom villas spread out with own plunge pool, all white and multilevel in the style of a southern Spanish development. Tennis and watersports, on a much-improved beach, honeymoon, family, diving packages. The food is good, international and aimed at pleasing everybody, families well catered for.

$$$ The Boiled Frog
Choc Bay, T758-720 8843, www.theboiledfrog.net.
Canadian-owned 2-room guesthouse by the beach with supermarket, bank, buses the other side of the road. Good location within easy reach of both Castries and Rodney Bay. Comfortable rooms with great view from deck. Evening meals can be taken with the family and their dog or **The Wharf** is just along the sand.

$$ Golden Arrow Inn
Gablewoods Mall, on highway to Gros Islet, T758-450 1832, http://goldenarrowinnslu.com.
Simple, pleasant rooms, private bathroom, modern house with balcony and veranda, view down to the bay. Within walking distance of beach and bus, friendly host, complimentary breakfast, **Golden Sun** restaurant and bar on the property, parking.

Rodney Bay *p40, map p41*

$$$$ Coco Palm
Rodney Bay Blvd, T758-456 2800, www.coco-resorts.com.
Excellent location close to beach, restaurants, nightlife and other activities within a stone's throw. A variety of comfortable rooms and prices in 2 sections, the more expensive block set back from the road is quieter, good for families or couples, all-inclusive and other packages available, reasonably priced restaurant, spa. Friendly service.

$$$$-$$$ Bay Gardens
Rodney Bay, T758-457 8006, www.baygardensresorts.com.
The resort comprises 3 hotels: **Beach Resort**, **Hotel** and **Inn**, catering for families, couples and business travellers. The flagship property is the **Beach Resort**, with a great location on Reduit Beach. rooms and suites which can be connected to make 2-bedroom apartments, wheelchair accessibility, smart and upmarket, security staff on the beach deter hustlers. The 2 other properties in the village are convenient and comfortable.

$$$$-$$$ Harmony Suites
Southern end of Rodney Bay marina with waterfront docking, T758-452 8756, www.harmonysuites.com.
Small, pleasant hotel, locally owned and managed. 30 suites, classic, premium and luxury waterfront, with kitchenettes, also **Cockpit Bistro**.

$$$$-$$$ Ginger Lily
T758-458 0300, www.gingerlilyhotel.com.
Small hotel with spacious rooms and suites conveniently located right opposite **Spinnakers**, the police station and the beach.

$$$ La Terrasse
T758-5720389, www.la terrassestlucia.com.
Colourful 4-room guesthouse attached to a French restaurant, rooms of different sizes, 2 of them share a bathroom, 2 have en suites. Can be noisy at weekends as behind nightclub, take earplugs, but otherwise friendly and good value, close to beach, restaurants and shops.

North Coast *p43, map p32*

$$$-$$ Bay Guest House
Bay St, Gros Islet, T758-450 8956, www.bay-guesthouse.com.
Minimum stay 2 nights, spacious rooms, studio with kitchenette or apartment with kitchen, painted bright orange, on waterfront, beside a beach, run by knowledgeable Will and Stephanie, an English/French couple, and their dogs.

$$$-$$ Henry's La Panache
Cas-en-Bas Rd, Gros Islet, T758-450 0765, www.lapanache.com.
Run by Henry Augustin, helpful and friendly, and Roger Graveson, a botanist (www.saintlucianplants.com), information on Atlantic beaches and coastal walking, birdwatching tours. Simple self-catering accommodation on hillside with good view in 2 studio apartments and a 2-bedroom apartment, all with balcony, bathroom, fridge, cooking facilities, insect screens, fans, gardens with plants labelled, breakfast packs US$5, library, parking. Holiday apartments in the south also available for an affordable 2-centre holiday.

$$$-$$ Tropical Breeze
38 Massie St, Massade, Gros Islet, T758-450 0589, www.tropicalbreezeresorts.com.
Guesthouse with bedrooms only or 1- to 4-bedroomed apartments, fully equipped, kitchens, group rates on request. Breakfast and other meals available, St Lucian cooking, discounts for long stays. Modern white building overlooking Rodney Bay, backs on to police station and is within easy reach of buses, the cricket ground or the venues for the Jazz Festival.

$$ Italian Guesthouse
Haxted Rd, Gros Islet, T758-716 8558.
Perched on hillside with great view over Rodney Bay and Pigeon Island, 11 studios and self-contained apartments sleep 1-4, some have kitchens, wood and stone bungalows, communal barbecue, complimentary laundry service, lovely gardens, hammocks, hot tub, helpful housekeeper.

East coast to Vieux Fort *p44, map p32*

$$$ Zamacá
15 Fond Bay Dr, Micoud, T758-454 1309, www.zamacastlucia.com.
Smart and clean, Ellen and John offer excellent hospitality and very good food, comfortable rooms, relaxing atmosphere.

$$$-$$ Foxgrove Inn
Mon Repos, T758-455 3271,
www.foxgroveinn.com.
On hillside with wonderful view of
Praslin Bay and Fregate Islands, this
Swiss/St Lucian-owned hotel is just by
Mamiku Gardens. It has 12 bedrooms,
a 1-bedroom and a 2-bedroom
apartment, ask for view to front, nothing
fancy but comfortable, large pool, nature
trails, good food, breakfast included,
meal plans available, discounts for long
stay, German and French spoken, a good
base for exploring the east coast.

Vieux Fort *p48, map p32*

$$$ Villa Caribbean Dream
Moule à Chique, T758-454 6846,
www.caribdreams.net.
Pretty, Créole-style guesthouse with
4 rooms in main house with shared
bathrooms and communal kitchen or
bungalow apartment in the garden
with view up the coast to the Pitons.
Wonderful breakfasts, other meals
available. Brigitte (German) is incredibly
helpful and hospitable.

$$ The Reef
Anse de Sables, T758-454 3418,
www.slucia.com/reef.
4 double or twin rooms in rustic wooden
cabins behind the café under the sea
grape trees, no sea view, solar-heated
hot water, private bathrooms, fans,
mosquito nets, breakfast included at the
café on the beach.

West coast to Soufrière *p48, map p32*

$$$$ The Inn On the Bay
Marigot Bay, T758-451 4260,
www.saint-lucia.com.
Only 5 rooms, spacious, in a white
West Indian-style building with

wrap-around balconies up on the hill
overlooking Marigot Bay, great view
from pool and balcony, continental
breakfast included with pastries, cereal
and fruit, tours and car hire arranged,
complimentary transport down to the
bay, run by friendly Normand Viau and
Louise Boucher.

$$$$ Ti Kaye Resort & Spa
Just south of Anse La Raye,
T758-456 8101, www.tikaye.com.
Romantic and popular for weddings
and honeymoons. White wooden
cottages with decorative fretwork, large
verandas with rocking chairs and double
hammocks. Outside showers, large
bedroom with louvred windows. Some
rooms have own plunge pool. Main
pool by bar and restaurant, good food
and extensive cocktail list (Piton Snow
recommended: white rum, triple sec,
coconut cream, frozen). 169 steps down
the cliff to pretty Anse Cochon beach
and 2nd restaurant.

$$$$-$$ Marigot Beach Club
On the north shore of Marigot bay, T758-
451 4974, www.marigotbeachclub.com.
Waterfront **Doolittle's** restaurant and
bar, live entertainment most nights, steel
bands. Lots of activities including sailing,
kayaking, PADI dive shop, pool, sundeck,
beach, gaming room. Studios with
kitchenette, fans, bathrooms and patio
or very pretty, light and airy villas with
1-3 bedrooms on hillside.

$$$ JJ's Paradise
T758-451 4076, jjsparadise@hotmail.com.
Cabins on hillside in lush gardens with
fruit trees and banana plants, simple
rooms, waterfront café below for meals.

$$$$ Anse Chastanet Resort and Jade Mountain
T758-459 7000, www.ansechastanet. com, www.jademountainstlucia.com.
Hilltop, hillside and beachside suites, all different but all really special, from wooden-lodge style to white-Spanish style and then the Jade Mountain suites with every facility including an infinity pool, concierge service, romantic, luxurious, stunning views in all directions, open balconies, airy. The best scuba diving on the island, consistently highly rated dive operation, diving packages available, watersports, tennis, jungle biking, 2 spas, lovely setting, restaurants on the beach and halfway up the hill, live music in the evenings, walks and excursions available, isolated.

$$$$ Boucan Hotel & Restaurant
Rabot Estate, T758-572 9600, www.hotelchocolat.com/uk/boucan.
Modern chic on old colonial cocoa plantation 300 m up overlooking Petit Piton with fabulous views. Lodges have every comfort and outdoor showers. Daily shuttle down to hotel boat for visiting different beaches. Spa with everything cocoa themed. Restaurant with every dish cocoa themed. Bean to bar tour of the property and making your own chocolate.

$$$$ Crystals
Colombette, overlooking Soufrière, T758-384 8995, www.stlucia crystals.com.
5 cottages and a villa in lush hillside gardens with exceptional view of sea and Pitons, rustic outside but every luxury inside, 1-3 a/c bedrooms, full kitchen, each has a sun deck and a plunge pool, swimming pool or jacuzzi.

Complimentary orientation tour of Soufrière for new arrivals. Tree top bar suspended in 5 mango trees with view of Pitons, great for sunset cocktails on the deck, sociable hosts and guests. Restaurant for guests only, meals on request.

$$$$ Fond Doux Holiday Plantation
Soufrière, T758-459 7545, www.fonddoux estate.com.
Traditional old colonial house and newer gingerbread cottages dotted around the estate between fruit and palm trees, comfortably furnished with polished wooden floors. Now 12 cottages, 2 restaurants and spa. Gorgeous setting in a tranquil and beautiful landscape with trails for walking around the estate.

$$$$ La Dauphine Estate
See Villa Beach Cottages page 59, for contact details).
A 4-bedroom Great House (sleeps 10) and 2-bedroom Chateau Laffitte on a 200-acre plantation 5 miles from Soufrière. Built in 1890 in gingerbread style, surrounded by lush gardens and hills, refurbished to modern standards, housekeeper/cook provided, good hiking along nature trails and through fruit plantation.

$$$$ Ladera Resort
T758-459 7323, www.ladera.com.
Spectacular setting between Gros Piton and Petit Piton, 1000 ft up, luxury suites, each lacking a west wall over a drop that only Superman could climb, providing an uninterrupted view of the Pitons, every luxury, plunge pools or pools with waterfalls, used to film *Superman II*, lots of birds and mosquitoes.

$$$$ Stonefield Estate Resort
T758-459 7037,
www.stonefieldresort.com.
Small hillside villa resort, romantic, with stunning views of Petit Piton and overlooking Malgretoute Beach. Villas sleep 2-8 with outdoor showers, kitchens, hammocks on the veranda and many have plunge pools. Spa treatments use local and organic products. A 26-acre former cocoa estate, the grounds are forested, with many fruit trees and birds and a nature trail to some petroglyphs, which are the resort's logo. Good restaurant, but a shuttle will take you to Soufrière if you want to shop for food. Fruit from the estate is complimentary.

$$$$ Sugar Beach
T758-456 8000,
www.viceroyhotelsandresorts.com/
sugarbeach.
Formerly the **Jalousie Plantation**. On a greatly improved beach between the Pitons, built in colonial style with a faux Great House as the central reception and dining area and luxury rooms in gingerbread cottages or sugar mill style. Amazing tree house spa incorporating original sugar mill walls. Owned by Roger Myers, former accountant to the Rolling Stones, whose collection of rock and other art decorates the **Cane Bar**, a speciality rum bar.

$$$$-$$$ La Haut
T758-459 7008, www.lahaut.com.
Family-run inn with pleasant rooms, excellent food and drinks (see below), all reasonably priced, free beach shuttle, friendly service. Best of all, though, is the view of the Pitons, breathtaking from anywhere on the property but especially from the infinity pool.

$$$ Chez Camille
7 Bridge St, T758-459 5379, www.cavip.
com/en/hotels/chezcamille.html.
Older-style house with wrap-around balcony and St Lucian decor and furnishings. Clean and friendly, 5 rooms, family room available. Kitchen for guests' use or the maid can cook for you, good restaurant attached where guests get 10% discount (does takeaways).

$$ La Mirage Guesthouse
14 Church St, T758-459 7010.
English owner of Jamaican descent, Gilroy Lamontaigne, 4 rooms sleep 3, bathroom, fan and fridge, lounge with cable TV, restaurant.

The Southwest *p48*

$$$ Balenbouche Estate
T758-455 1244, www.balenbouche.com.
Austrian-born Uta Lawaetz and her daughters care for this heritage site and their guests with simplicity and intuition. The 19th-century plantation house and the four cottages, sleeping 2-4, are furnished with antiques, surrounded by enormous old trees, mature gardens and the remains of a sugar mill and water wheel. Its tranquillity makes it ideal as a yoga retreat, but families are equally happy here. Wonderful food from the organic farm on the 30-ha estate. 2 small beaches within short walk along paths through the gardens.

$$$ Mirage Beach
Laborie, T758-455 9237,
www.miragestlucia.com.
2 apartments or rent the whole house, right on the beach in a fishing community where you can get to know village life. There are restaurants nearby or local cooks can prepare meals in your apartment if you don't want to cook.

Restaurants

Castries *p31, map p34*

$$$ Brown Sugar
Vigie Cove, T758-458 1931, www. brownsugarrestaurantandbar.com. Tue-Sun 1100-1430, 1900-2300, bar open all day, happy hour 1700-1900.
Open-air waterfront restaurant in a lovely garden with a view of the harbour and all the boats coming and going. Family-run with attention to detail and excellent service. International menu with local touches, good, hearty food.

$$$ Coal Pot
Vigie Marina, T758-452 5566, www.coalpotrestaurant.com. Mon-Fri 1200-1445, 1830-2145, Sat dinner only, closed Sun.
The place to eat, outstanding, reservations essential. A very romantic, candlelit interior with beautiful artwork or terrace dining overlooking the marina. Sophisticated international cuisine, delicious fresh food with all the trimmings, accompanied by a good wine list.

$$$ Pink Plantation House
Chef Harry Drive, The Morne, T758-452 5422. Mon-Thu 1130-1500, Fri 1130-2100, Sun 0900-1200.
The limited opening hours mean that reservations are recommended. Owned by a ceramicist, Michelle Elliot, you can pop in to her workshop and buy her pottery. Tables on the verandah of this traditional wooden colonial house with pretty fretwork and shuttered windows enjoy a lovely view through a beautiful garden on the hillside overlooking Castries harbour. Tasty food, substantial Sun brunch, friendly service, a very pleasant experience.

$ Flamingo
William Peter Blvd. Open until about 1600, closes about 1200 on Sat.
Favourite local place for a cheeseburger or roti, for a chicken roti specify if you want it without skin and bones.

$ Kimlans
Derek Walcott Square, T758-452 1136. Mon-Sat 0700-2300.
Upstairs café and bar with veranda, cheap, serves local food. A chicken and potato roti washed down with a local juice overlooking the square will renew your energy for sightseeing. Good place for people watching.

North of Castries *p39, map p32*

$$$-$$ The Wharf
Choc Bay, short distance past Gablewoods Mall, T758-450 4844. Daily 0900-2400, happy hour 1800-1900.
Beach setting, casual, sandwiched between the road and the sea, waiter service to your sunbed, varied menu, reasonable prices, international comfort food such as burgers and club sandwiches but with a local twist: banana ketchup or hot sauce, or local cuisine such as roti, crab backs, fish cakes and accra. Good set meal of soup, fish or chicken and dessert for about US$9 or you can splash out on shrimp or beef tenderloin. Lively in the evenings, restaurant, bar and dancing, karaoke, soul, salsa, live music Sat. Great rum cocktails.

$$ Miss Saigon
Gablewoods Mall, T758-451 7309. Breakfast, lunch and dinner.
Serves full English breakfast, Chinese and Oriental food for other meals. St Lucians who work in the area come here for lunch.

$ Friends Café and Patisserie
Casa St Lucia, Vigie, T758-458 1335.
Mon-Thu 0730-1900, Fri, Sat 0900-2100.
Patisserie and café, very good
sandwiches, good midday meal but you
have to get there early to make sure of
getting it, attractive, lovely walk from
here to the Vigie lighthouse.

Rodney Bay *p40, map p41*

$$$ Big Chef
T758-450 0210, www.bigchef steakhouse.
com. Open daily 1800-2300.
Tender, tasty Angus steaks, at around
US$35-40 depending on the weight,
also lobster in season. Very popular and
with good reason, the food is delicious.
Comfortable dining with friendly,
efficient service. Behind the restaurant,
on the waterfront with a dinghy dock, is
Tapas on the Bay (*same ownership, T758-
451 2433, Mon-Sat 1100-2300, happy hour
1600-1800*), with a good range of tapas
from around US$6, accompanied by a
short but appropriate selection of sherry,
Spanish or world wines available by the
glass for US$7.50, also cocktails. Lovely
setting with Wi-Fi.

$$$ Buzz
Opposite Royal St Lucia, T758-458 0450,
http://buzzstlucia.com. 1700-late, closed
Mon, Sun brunch in season.
Seafood and grill, local and international
dishes, lobster, Moroccan-spiced lamb
shanks, shepherd's pie, pepperpot and
a few vegetarian options. Reservations
recommended unless you are prepared
to wait an hour or more. Indoor or
outdoor seating, even indoors is very
open and airy with shutters raised, blue
and lemon yellow decor in West Indian-
style building, smart but comfortable.
Live music Fri from 1900, often a
saxophonist plays.

$$$ Charthouse
Overlooking the lagoon, by Reduit Beach,
T758-452 8115. Mon-Sat 1800-2230.
Open-air restaurant, a room without
walls overlooking the yachts. Known for
its prime US beef, particularly the roast
rib, as well as steak, lobster, seafood
and spare ribs, excellent rib steak,
Cuban cigars. Accompaniments often of
lower quality and generally considered
overpriced.

$$$ Elegance Café
Massade, T758-450 9864, www.
facebook.com/Elegancecafesaintlucia.
Mon-Sat lunch and dinner.
Excellent Indian cuisine, beautifully
presented and with excellent service,
see Facebook for weekly specials.
They also do more international menu
items such as some great burgers and
vegetable juices. Reasonably priced and
good value.

**$$$ Fire Grill Steak House and
Lounge Bar**
Reduit Beach Av, T758-451 4745, see
Facebook, dinner 1800-2300, bar until
0100.
Where all the food, whether steak, fish
or seafood is cooked over the fire, main
courses from US$15, a 14-oz rib eye
steak US$45 and Sat night lobster US$35,
family friendly, weekly live jazz and
blues, comfy leather sofas in the lounge
bar, huge selection of rums.

$$$ Jacques Waterfront Dining
Rodney Bay Village, T758-458 1900,
www.jacques restaurant.com.
Daily 1200-1500, 1800-2200.
Waterfront bistro at the end of Reduit
Beach overlooking the entrance to
the marina, formerly Froggie Jacques,
relocated from Vigie after a fire. French
and Caribbean cuisine, all beautifully

presented, one of the best restaurants. Run by French chef, Jacques Rioux. Reservations recommended.

$$$ Memories of Hong Kong
Opposite Royal St Lucian Hotel, T758-452 8218. Mon-Sat 1700-2230.
A breezy location with fairy lights and lanterns around the veranda and tables. Chinese chef from Hong Kong, good but pricey food.

$$$ Razmataz
Opposite Royal St Lucian, T758-452 9800, www.razmatazrestaurant.com. Fri-Wed from 1700, happy hour 1700-1900.
Indian, chefs from Nepal, good, wide range of dishes, particularly good for vegetarians, very popular with British clientele, friendly, on Sat a belly dancer weaves her way around the diners.

$$$ Spice of India
Bay Walk Mall, Rodney Bay Village, T758-458 4243, http://spiceofindiastlucia.com. Open Tue-Sun 1200-1545, 1800-late.
Indian chefs use Indian ingredients as well as local produce such as seafood for an authentic flavour. See Facebook for tasting lunch menus. Very popular with both St Lucians and tourists, reservations recommended.

$$$-$$ Key Largo
Rodney Heights, T758-452 0282.
Wood oven-baked pizzas, good thin crust, pasta dishes, salads, cold beer, outside tables and small trampolines for children.

$$$-$$ Spinnakers
Directly on the beach at Reduit, T758-452 8491, http://spinnakersbeachbar.com. Breakfast, lunch and dinner daily from 0900, happy hour 1700-1800.
Long-established, unpretentious beach bar, excellent location, though food and service suffer when it is busy. Lots of variety on the menu, dinner is different from lunch, when there are salads, panini, burgers, as well as fish and meat dishes, most of which are US$9-17, although lobster mayonnaise is US$45.

$$ Breadbasket
At the marina, T758-452 0647. Breakfast, lunch and dinner.
A favourite for breakfast and great rotis, sandwiches and pastries. Good-value lunches and a nice spot to sit and watch the action in the marina.

$$ The Lime
T758-452 0761. Open 1100-1400, 1830-0100.
Friendly, casual, open air, serves good cafeteria-style meals popular at lunch with locals when there is usually a meat or vegetarian dish of the day, large portions, also rotis and snacks at moderate prices.

$$-$ Café Olé
Rodney Bay Marina, T758-452 8726. Open daily.
Freshly made baguettes, salads, light meals, desserts, a popular coffee shop.

$$-$ Elena's
Rodney Bay Marina, T758-723 8800. Daily 0800-2200, ice cream from 0900.
Elena has several ice cream parlours using fresh fruits and natural ingredients, but has now expanded with a pizzeria and café. Great breakfasts with lots of choice, pizza baked in wood-fired oven for lunch and supper or takeaway, also good salads.

Pigeon Island *p42*

$$$-$$ Jambe de Bois
T758-458 0728/ 452 0321. From breakfast until 2130 except Mon when it closes at 1700.
Rustic, wooden furniture with seating outside or inside. The stone walls are in the style of the military buildings and the roof is thatched. Serves reasonably priced meals, offering baguettes, fish, soup, cakes, salads, art gallery, book swap, post cards. On Sat evening there is a jazz group, around 1830-2130, very pleasant to sit at the tables on the deck at the water's edge.

North coast *p43, map p32*

$$$-$$ Marjorie's Beach Bar
Cas-en-Bas, T758-520 0001.
Typical wooden beach bar with a wood-tiled roof, picnic tables outside or tables under cover, beach loungers for long-stay customers, gift shacks around the edge, great to sit with a beer and watch the kitesurfers in the bay. Daily menu on the board for lunch. Check if Miss Marjorie is open for dinner as she sometimes closes, but will usually open if you tell her in advance what you want to eat or how much you want to pay. Cash only, no credit cards.

East coast to Vieux Fort *p44, map p32*

$$$-$$ Whispering Palm
Foxgrove Inn, Mon Repos, T758-455 3800, www.foxgroveinn.com. Breakfast, lunch and dinner.
Spectacular view from balcony of restaurant over Praslin Bay and the Atlantic Ocean. Very good food, try the smoked fish or smoked duck salad for a delicious lunch, washed down with a local juice such as guava or passion fruit.

Main dishes include fish, steak or pasta. Good place to stop during a tour of the east coast.

Vieux Fort *p48, map p32*

$$-$ The Old Plantation Yard
Lower Commercial St, T758-454 6040, oldplant@hotmail.com.
Lots of history, laid-back atmosphere, gorgeous Créole food and local drinks. A good place to eat before going to the airport. Try the fresh lime juice on a hot day and lunch on local specialities such as crab back and dumplings in season. Limited menu options but all fresh and local. Mini **Jazz Festival** held here at the beginning of May.

$$-$ The Reef Beach Café
Anse de Sables beach, T758-454 3418, www.slucia.com/reef. Tue-Sun 0800-2200, Mon 0800-1800.
Pleasant bar with glorious view over bay to Maria Islands with kitesurfers for added interest, local drinks and delicacies, milk shakes and cocktails, seafood, fish and chips, roti, pizza, burgers and baguettes, reasonable prices, tables out by the beach under sea grape trees as well as inside the building. Wi-Fi.

West coast to Soufrière *p48, map p32*

$$$ Marsala Bay
Marigot Bay Marina Village at Capella Resort, T758-451 4500. Dinner only, 1800-2200.
The same ownership and chef as Spice of India in Rodney Bay, serving Indian and Indo-Chinese (*hakka*) cuisine on the waterfront. Delicious food and very popular. Takeaway available if you are on a yacht or self-catering, Wi-Fi, caters for special diets.

$$$ Rainforest Hideaway
Marigot Bay, T758-286 0511,
www.rainforesthideawaystlucia.com.
Beautiful decor and setting, built out
over the water. Take the free ferry across
from the jetty by the police/customs
building. Good food, fusion European
Caribbean, à la carte or prix fixe menu,
US$48 for 2 courses, US$59 for 3,
including amuse bouche and sorbet,
plus 10% VAT and 10% service. Live jazz
Mon, Wed, Thu, Sat.

$$$-$$ Chateau Mygo House of Seafood
Marigot Bay, T758-458 3947.
Daily 0700-2300.
Waterfront bar and grill. Serves
traditional hot bakes and cocoa tea for
breakfast, seafood and sushi, thin crust
pizzas from US$8, credit cards accepted,
reservations advised, live music and
dancing weekly.

$$$-$$ Roots Bar
Marigot Bay, T758-721 5182.
Mon 1200-1800, Tue-Fri, Sun 1100-1900.
Great beach bar run by Sue and Fluffy,
who are friendly and helpful, catering for
vegetarians and allergy sufferers using
local cuisine and offering a cold Piton
beer to wash it down.

Soufrière *p50, map p32*

$$$ Boucan
Hotel Chocolat at Rabot Estate, T758-
5729600, www.hotelchocolat.com/uk/
boucan. Breakfast 0700-1000, lunch
1200-1500 and dinner 1800-2130.
Modern and chic, open with a
glorious view of the Pitons. Innovative
creations with a chocolate theme for
savoury and sweet dishes, using local
cocoa and other local ingredients.

A great experience. Barbecue evening
once a week.

$$$ Dasheene
Ladera Resort, T758-459 7323. Breakfast
for hotel guests only, lunch 1130-1430,
and dinner 1830-2130.
Up on a hillside, 300 m above sea level,
wonderful views of the Pitons, worth
coming here even if only for a drink
just for the views. Caribbean Créole,
mostly produce from local farmers
and fishermen used as well as some
international delicacies.

$$$ Orlando's
Cemetery Rd, Fond Bernier,
Soufrière, T758-459 5955,
www.orlandosrestaurantstl.com.
Daily for breakfast 0730-1000, Wed-Mon
1200-2100, Tue 1400-2100.
On the main road before the bridge
coming into town, chef Orlando Sachell
is at the helm of this Caribbean gourmet
restaurant. Small garden setting, 2
multi-course prix fixe tasting menus
with small portions of each course, or
normal menu choices. Good fish and
chips, which is mahi mahi with sweet
potato chips, generally using locally
sourced ingredients from farmers and
fishermen in the area. A good lunch stop
on an island tour, reservations advised.
Service is attentive and Orlando greets
all dinner guests.

$$$-$$ Delice Restaurant & Bar
La Haut Plantation, on the west coast
road 1.5 miles north of Soufrière, T758-
459 7008, www.lahaut.com. 0730-1030,
1130-1530, 1700-2100.
Excellent lunch with some unusual items
such as pumpkin chips, crêpes and rotis,
dinner also delicious with good wine list,
stunning views of Pitons and Sulphur
Springs, also rooms.

$$$-$$ The Humming Bird
On the beach, north end of
Soufrière, T758-459 7232,
www.hummingbirdbeachresort.com/.
Open from 0700.
A nice place to eat and take a swim.
French, Créole and seafood, daily
specials, varied menu, fish, steak,
surf'n'turf, vegetarian meals, lunchtime
salads and sandwiches, good but
expensive, good views of the town and
Petit Piton. Créole night Wed with live
music and dancing. Also a hotel.

$$$-$$ Mango Tree
Stonefield Estate Villa Resort, *T758-*
459 7037, www.stone fieldresort.com.
Daily 0730-2200.
Gorgeous setting overlooking Petit Piton
and Malgretoute beach and great for
sunset watching. Serving breakfast, lunch
and dinner, the menu is wide ranging,
with some vegetarian dishes as well as
the usual seafood, meat and pasta. A
barbecue on Thu with limbo dancing,
fire eating and DJ music is usually heavily
booked, so even guests have to make
reservations. Live steel pan music Sun.

$$-$ Martha's Tables
Malgretout, Jalousie Rd,
T758-459 7270, www.marthastables.
com. Mon-Fri 1130-1500.
Home-style cooking, Créole fish, chicken,
vegetarian dishes, rice and peas, ground
provisions, lots of choice of local food
eaten at mismatched tables and chairs
under lean-to roof, or meals to go. Credit
cards accepted.

The southwest *p56, map p32*

$$$-$$ Debbie's Place
Saphire Estate, Laborie, T758-455 1625.
Sizeable portions of tasty Créole food
with lots of trimmings and side dishes, to

eat in or takeaway, buffet lunch on Sun.
Lots of car parking space.

Bars and clubs

Most of St Lucia's nightlife revolves
around the hotels, while some
restaurants host live bands. Bars and
clubs are concentrated around Rodney
Bay, all within easy walking distance
of each other, although there is plenty
of nightlife in Marigot Bay too. Some
have strict entry restrictions on age
and dress, so check beforehand.
They offer a mix of live bands and DJs
playing regional and international
music. See also box, page 70.

Castries *p31, map p34*

Prio's Country Palace
Upstairs, above the market.
Sat night country and western music and
dance, very popular, taken very seriously
but great fun. The love of country and
western dates from the Second World
War, when American soldiers brought
their music to their bases and locals
perceived a similarity to their traditional
cuadrille. Go and watch the courtly
dancing even if you don't join in. Great
foot work. Vendors outside sell chicken,
rum and beer.

Rodney Bay *p40, map p41*

Antillia Brewing Company
4 Seagrape Av, T758-458 0844,
see Facebook.
For an alternative to Piton beer, this craft
brewer is now producing Golden Wheat,
Pale Ale, Stout and seasonal ales, no
chemicals or preservatives added. Beers
on tap, happy hour 1700-1900, sold in
6 oz, 12 oz and 16 oz measures. Free
Wi-Fi, pub food, plenty of room with

Entertainment on St Lucia

St Lucia is not great for the arts and entertainment as its culture has developed in other ways. While there are several major poets and playwrights on the island (such as the Nobel Laureate Derek Walcott) and everybody loves **music** and **dance**, theatre as such is rather ad hoc or geared to specific festivals, usually on an annual basis. There are (irregular) shows: concerts, drama, dance, comedy, at the National Cultural Centre (Castries), the Light House Theatre (Tapion) and occasionally at the Great House Theatre (Cap Estate). They can give you a better taste of St Lucian culture than hotel shows.

Rodney Bay is the place to head for live music and dance, where bars and clubs are all within easy walking distance of each other (see Bars and clubs, below). Hotels also lay on entertainment and are a frequent venue for steel pan music, folk dancing, crab racing, fire eating, limbo dancing and mock carnival singing and dancing. The hotels welcome guests from outside, but this might not be the authentic St Lucia experience you are looking for.

The big event is the annual **Jazz Festival** In May, which dominates the music scene with lots of outdoor concerts. Both St Lucian and international musicians are invited and there are opportunities to hear zouk, reggae and other music forms as well as jazz.

For more informal entertainment there are street parties. Friday nights are big for going out and St Lucians enjoy eating fresh local food while

seating indoors by the bar or outside on the wrap-around verandah.

Delirius
Reduit Beach Av opposite Coco Kreole, T758-451 3354, www.deliriusstlucia.com. Mon-Sat until late.
Lively, contemporary bar on the main street, lots of cocktails using local ingredients, award-winning bartender, live music some nights, DJs Wed, Fri, Sat, see Facebook for what's on. Also restaurant Mon-Sat serving mostly seafood, yacht provisioning and deliveries of ready meals for self-catering visitors. For a crawl of the bars and clubs on this strip, next to Delirius are **Gravity**, **Rehab**, and **Turbulence**, while **The Hairy Clam** is behind them, with an outdoor bar and loud music.

Treasure Bay Casino
Baywalk Mall, www.treasurebaystlucia. com, daily 1300-0100.
St Lucia's only casino. Table games, slots, video poker, sports bar with 28 big screen TVs. No dress code and no ID required, very casual.

Festivals

Jan The last week in Jan is **Nobel Laureate Week**, with lectures celebrating the 2 Nobel prize winners produced by the island (Sir Arthur Lewis and Derek Walcott). They were both born on 23 Jan.

22 Feb Independence Day is celebrated extensively. There is a large exhibition lasting several days from the various ministries, business and industry, socializing in the open air, known as liming, followed by music and dancing, known as a jump-up. The highlight of the week is **Seafood Friday**, at Anse La Raye, just south of Castries, where you can get the cheapest and freshest lobster on the island in season and fish at any time of year. The entire street running parallel to the bay has chairs and tables under awnings, serving seafood of your choice. However it is so popular that food tends to run out by 2100, so get there early. Everyone is very friendly and there is no hassling. Music is at a bearable pitch and sometimes you can hear a local quadrille band. If you are on the east coast, you can try **Dennery** for fish-on-the-beach at weekends, 1600-0200, while **Sware**, Vieux Fort, is a lively Friday street party where you can eat unlimited fish accompanied by the beat of local music.

Alternatively, head for the **jump-up** from 2200 at Gros Islet, where it is hard to resist getting involved. If you haven't eaten beforehand, or if you work up another appetite, you can get barbecued chicken legs, lambi/conch, accra (fish cakes) and floats from the street stalls. The mix of tourists to St Lucians is weighted heavily towards the former, but it can be enjoyable nonetheless if you are a night owl who likes music and dancing. There can be more hassling here and you should stay away from anyone offering drugs.

Sunset cruises are a good way of winding down after a busy day on the beach. Boats usually travel down the west coast and serve champagne, rum cocktails or soft drinks to help you spot the elusive green flash as the sun dips below the horizon.

and NGOs, such as the National Trust, and various sporting events, serious discussions and musical programmes. **May** The annual **St Lucia Jazz & Arts Festival** is now an internationally recognized event, drawing large crowds every year. Most concerts are open-air and take place in the evening, although fringe events are held anywhere, anytime, with local bands playing in Castries at lunchtime. As well as jazz, played by international stars, you can hear Latin, salsa, soca and zouk, steel drums or reggae. For more details T758-451 8566, http://stluciajazz.org. You can buy a single ticket or a season pass. Tickets available online or at the Department of Culture and **Sunshine Bookstore** (Gablewoods Mall).

29 Jun **St Peter's Day** is celebrated as the **Fisherman's Feast**, in which all the fishing boats are decorated.
Jul **Carnival** is a high point, when colourful bands and costumed revellers make up processions through the streets. There is lots of music, dancing and drinking. Everything goes on for hours, great stamina is required to keep going. On the Sat are the calypso finals, on Sun the King and Queen of the band followed by J'ouvert at 0400 until 0800 or 0900. On Mon and Tue the official parades of the bands take place. Most official activities take place at Marchand Ground but warming-up parties and concerts are held all over the place. Tue night there is another street party.
30 Aug **Feast of the Rose of Lima** (*Fét La Wòz*). Members of the societies gather

in various public places around the island to dance and sing in costume.

Oct The 1st Mon is **Thanksgiving**, held either to give thanks for no hurricane or for survival of a hurricane.

17 Oct **La Marguerite**, a festival to rival the Rose with a church service, parade with participants dressed as kings and queens, officers and members of the court, then lots of music, food and drink. Both festivals have their origins in the secret societies formed by slaves under French and British colonial rule. **Jounen Kwéyòl Entensyonnal** (International Créole Day), on the last Sun, although activities are held throughout the month. 4 or 5 rural communities are selected for the celebration. There is local food, craft, music and different cultural shows. Expect traffic jams everywhere as people visit venues across the island. A lot is in Kwéyòl/patois, but you will still have a good time and a chance to sample mouth-watering local food.

Nov **22 Nov** **St Cecilia's Day**, the patron saint of musicians is celebrated in Roman Catholic churches.

End-Nov **Atlantic Rally for Cruisers**, an annual transatlantic competition for cruising yachts, starting in Las Palmas, Gran Canaria in November and ending before Christmas in Rodney Bay. Covering 2700 nautical miles, it is the largest sailing event in the world and over 200 boats of different shapes and sizes take part, culminating in parties and more parties in St Lucia.

Dec **13 Dec** **St Lucy's Day** used to be called **Discovery Day**, but as Columbus' log shows he was not in the area at that time, it was renamed. It is now known as **National Day**. St Lucy, the patron saint of light, is honoured during National Day by a procession of lanterns called the **Festival of Lights and Renewal**. For details contact **Castries City Council**, T758-452 2611 ext 7071.

Art and crafts

Bagshaw's, *La Toc, T758-452 2139*, also shops at La Place Carenage, Marigot and Windjammer Landing. **Silk screening studio** *(Mon-Fri 0830-1630, Sat 0830-1200)*. Take return air ticket for discount. **Eudovic's Art Studio**, *in Goodlands, coming down from the Morne heading south, T758-452 2747, www.eudovicart. com.* Local handicrafts and beautiful large wood carvings, studio and gallery.

Flowers

Garden Gate Flowers, *Bois D'Orange, T758-452 9176, www.tropicalislandflowers. com.* Takeaway boxes of ginger, heliconia, anthuriums, 48 hrs' notice required for export, pick up at airport or delivered to hotel, US$30-45.

Markets

Market day in **Castries** is Sat, very picturesque (much quieter on other days, speakers of Patois pay less than those who do not). A new public market has been built on the Castries waterfront, with the old market building renovated and turned into a craft market. Buy a coal-pot (native barbecue) and bring it home on your lap. **Soufrière** has a market on the waterfront, as does **Anse La Raye** along the seafront road, with tourist stalls selling clothing and souvenirs and a fish market. **Fisherman's Co-operative Market** on the John Compton Highway at the entrance to Pointe Seraphine. Fish is also sold inside the public market, good variety, hygienically displayed, and at an outlet outside the supermarket at JQ's Mall, Rodney Bay. Fishermen still sell their catch wherever they can. Fish is cheap and fresh.

Shopping malls

Baywalk Mall, *Rodney Bay, www. baywalkslu.com, Mon-Thu 0900-1900, Fri-Sat 0900-2000, Sun 0900-1400*. The newest and biggest mall on the island, housing designer fashion boutiques upstairs, **Sea Island Cotton Shop** (duty free), **Diamonds International**, **Digicel** and **Lime** phone companies, **Elena's Ice Cream**, **Spice of India**, **Church's Chicken**, **GL Foodmarket** (*Mon-Thu 0700-2200, Fri, Sat 0700-2400, Sun 0700-1800, T758-455 3663, www.glfoodmarket. com*), pharmacy, bank (*open Mon-Wed 0900-1600, Thu-Fri 0900-1800*) and 24-hr ATMs, as well as the casino.

Gablewoods Shopping Mall, *between Rodney Bay and Castries*, has a selection of boutiques, gift shops, book shop, post office, pharmacy, deli, open-air eating places and **Super J**.

JQ Mall at Rodney Bay, *www.shopjq mall.com. Mon-Thu 0900-1900, Fri, Sat 0900-2000, Sun 1000-1400)*. Less glitzy than Baywalk Mall opposite, with **Super J Supermarket** on the ground floor, clothing shops, souvenir and craft shops, pharmacy, bank, post office, **Sunshine Bookshop**, and fast food outlets.

La Place Carenage, *Jeremie St, Castries, T758-452 7318, www.carenagemall.com*. Duty-free shopping mall right by the cruise ships with jewellers, arts and crafts, clothing, places to eat, internet café, tour desk, taxi service, tourist information, car rental.

The Desmond Skeete Animation Center, *3rd floor, Jeremie St, Castries T758-453 2451*. A small historical museum with a 20-min light and sound show dramatizing St Lucia's history.

Pointe Seraphine, *next to the main port in Castries. Mon-Fri 0900-1600, Sat 0900-1400*. Ferry from La Place Carenage every 10 mins, US$1. Duty-free shopping centre, so take your airline ticket and passport, with many tourist-oriented outlets, restaurants, entertainment and tour operators. Goods bought here can be delivered directly to the airport. Cruise ships can tie up at the complex's own berths.

What to do

Cricket and football are the main spectator sports. Basketball, netball and volleyball are also popular. Every village has a cricket game at weekends or after work in the season, using makeshift equipment such as sticks or palm frond bases as bats. There is some excellent diving and snorkelling off the west coast and you can also fish, sail, windsurf and kitesurf and hire all manner of water toys. On land, there are acres of forest trails for hiking, biking and birdwatching as well as a good golf course and tennis courts at many of the hotels. For details, see Planning your trip, page 15.

Cricket

The **Beausejour Cricket Ground**, *T758-457 8834 (ticket office T758-450 8139)*, is the island's main stadium. Since its opening in 2002, it has hosted several Test and international matches including the 2007 World Cup. Benefiting from state-of-the-art technology, the 20,000-seater stadium has hospitality suites, a media centre and players' pavilion, and was the first ground in the West Indies to install floodlighting. The 4 stands are sponsored by local businesses.

Cycling

Bike St Lucia, *T758-457 1400, www. bikestlucia.com*. On Anse Mamin Plantation just north and part of the Anse Chastenet estate, they offer 8 miles of off-road riding on trails through forest (jungle biking). A guide takes you on a tour first, giving you a bit of history of the plantation and information about plants, then after one loop you go off on your own. Most of the trails are suitable for all levels; only Tinkers Trail is steep with roots and steps but the view from the top at over 300 m is worth the effort. The fleet of Cannondale bikes are not for use away from their trails. Accessible only by boat or from Anse Chastenet, they organize transfers from your hotel, boat from Castries (picking up cruise passengers), lunch, snorkelling, etc.

Palm Services Rainforest Cycling Adventure, *T758-458 0908, www. adventuretoursstlucia.com*. Hiking and cycling on the east coast through the forest up to the waterfall on Errard Plantation near Dennery. Popular cruise ship visitor excursion offered daily, while hotel guests are limited to Fri, Sat.

St Lucia Cycling Association, *see Facebook*, organizes road races, time trials and public fun rides. Cycling races are held on Independence Day starting at Castries market, with BMX, mountain bikes and road bikes and competitors of all ages.

Diving

For details of dive sites, see Planning your trip, page 16. Visitors must dive with a local company. It is illegal to take any coral or undersized shellfish. Corals and sponges should not even be touched. It is also illegal to buy or sell coral products on St Lucia. The **Soufrière Marine Management Association**, *www. smma.org.lc*, preserves the environment between Anse Chastanet and Anse L'Ivrogne to the south. It has placed moorings in the reserve, which yachts are required to take; charges are on a sliding scale depending on the size of the boat. Collection of marine mammals (dead or alive) is prohibited, spearguns are illegal and anchoring is prohibited. Rangers come by at night to collect the fee and explain the programme. Dive moorings have been installed and are being financed with **Marine Reserve Fees**, US$5 daily, US$15 a year for diving, US$1 for snorkelling. Dive companies charge 10% VAT on top of their quoted rates and often 10% service.

Dive Fair Helen, *Castries, T758-451 7716, www.divefairhelen.com*. 1 dive US$67.50, 2-dive package US$96, including transfers, lunch, mask, fins, snorkel, tanks and weight belt, PADI courses available, dive boats with wash room and shower and shade as well as platform and easy access to the water. Snorkelling and kayaking also offered.

Scuba St Lucia, *Anse Chastanet, Soufrière, T758-459 7755, www.scubastlucia. com, or contact them through the hotel*. PADI 5-star, SSI and DAN, the first and only dive centre to be accredited as a National Geographic Dive Center in the Windward Islands. Shore and boat dives. 3 dive boats with oxygen on each, photographic hire and film processing, video filming and courses, day and night dives, resort courses and full PADI certification, multilingual staff, pick-up service Mon-Sat from hotels north of Castries, day packages for divers, snorkellers, beginners and others include lunch and equipment.

Diving and marine life

There is some very good diving off the west coast of St Lucia, although this is somewhat dependent on the weather, as heavy rain tends to create high sediment loads in the rivers and sea. Diving off the east coast is not so good and can be risky unless you are a competent diver. One of the best beach entry dives in the Caribbean is directly off **Anse Chastanet**, where an underwater shelf drops off from about 10 ft down to 60 ft and there is a good dive over **Turtle Reef** in the bay, where there are over 25 different types of coral. Below the **Petit Piton** are impressive sponge and coral communities on a drop to 200 ft of spectacular wall. There are gorgonians, black coral trees, huge barrel sponges and plenty of other beautiful reef life. The area in front of the Anse Chastanet Hotel is a buoyed-off Marine Reserve, stretching from the west point at **Grand Caille North** to **Chamin Cove**. Only the hotel boats and local fishermen's canoes are allowed in. By the jetty, a roped-off area is used by snorkellers and beginner divers. Other popular dive sites include **Anse L'Ivrogne, Anse La Raye Point** (good snorkelling also at Anse La Raye) and the **Pinnacles** (an impressive site where four pinnacles rise to within 10 ft of the surface), not forgetting the wrecks, such as the *Volga* (in 20 ft of water north of Castries harbour, well broken up, subject to swell, requires caution), the *Waiwinette* (several miles south of Vieux Fort, strong currents, competent divers only), and the 165-ft *Lesleen M* (deliberately sunk in 1986 off Anse Cochon Bay in 60 ft of water).

Scuba Steve's Diving, *Rodney Bay Marina near the Fisheries Complex, T758-450 9433, www.scubastevesdiving. com*. 2 fast dive boats, take up to 12 or 15 divers, offers PADI courses, night dives and wreck dives.

Fishing
See Planning your trip, page 17.

Golf
St Lucia Golf & Country Club, *Cap Estate, T758-450 8523, www.stluciagolf. com*. A 6685-yd, par-71, 18-hole golf course and driving range, green fee US$95-105 for 9 holes, US$120-145 for 18 holes, depending on the time of year, golf carts mandatory. Club rental, Pro Shop, restaurant and group packages.

Hiking and birdwatching
For details of hiking trails, see Planning your trip, page 17. For the **National Park trails** a permit is required (usually US$10, half price for children), payable at the entrance or in advance. Guides are available at the start of most trails (Mon-Fri 0830-1500), or you can reserve one for a different time or at weekends for an extra charge; they are particularly useful if you want to set off early to sight birds at dawn, but they are not mandatory. Tours are often franchised to tour operators and a guide is certainly useful but organized tours are often noisy. Get your own permit from the Forestry Department if you feel confident about finding your own way.

Forestry Department, *www.malff. com*, organizes hiking across the island and has rangers who are specialized in finding birds. Contact the **Ecotourism Unit** (*T758-468 5648, sluforestrails@ hotmail.com*). For individual trails: **Union Trail** (*T758-468 5649*); **Vieux Fort office** (Des Cartiers Trail; *T758-454 5589*); **Millet Trail** (best for birdwatching; closed at the time of writing; *T758-451 1691*); **Forestierre Trail** (*T758-451 6168*); **Dennery Range** (Barre de l'Isle; *T758-716 6060*).

Rain Forest Adventures, *Chassin, T758-458 5151, www.rainforestadventure.com*. Has a guided 0600 birdwatching hike on the Jacquot Trail, 4-5 hrs.

St Lucia National Trust, *T758-452 5005*. Has fairly regular field trips, usually the last Sun of the month, popular with locals and tourists of all ages. The cost varies according to transport costs.

Kayaking

DFH Kayaking, *on the beach at Marigot Bay, T758-451 7716, www.dfhkayaking. com*. Tours Mon-Sat half day or full day, novice to advanced level. **Marigot Bay to Roseau River** is a combination of coastal, mangrove and river kayaking with snorkelling afterwards, US$70; kayaking at **Pigeon Island**, US$65; **Marigot Bay to Castries** includes snorkelling and the beach as well as sea kayaking, US$70; **Marigot Bay to Rat Island** is for more advanced kayakers and takes 4-6 hrs, depending on conditions, US$120; **Marigot Bay to Pigeon Island** (or vice versa), a full day trip including snorkelling and beach stops, US$145; **Marigot Bay to Anse Cochon** includes river, coastal, sea and mangrove kayaking, snorkelling, beach, lunch, a bit of everything, US$132, plus 10% VAT on all prices.

Kayak St Lucia, *Anse Chastenet, T758-459 0000, www.kayakstlucia. com*. Kayak tours to Soufrière and the Pitons or along Anse Mamin with a beach picnic, sunset kayaking or a birdwatching kayak tour early in the morning to see nesting seabirds.

Sailing

See also Planning your trip, page 18. At Marigot Bay and Rodney Bay you can hire any size of craft, the larger ones coming complete with crew if you want. Charters can be arranged to sail to neighbouring islands. Many of these yachts sail down to the Grenadines. **Rodney Bay** has been developed to accommodate 1000 yachts and hosts the annual **Atlantic Rally for Cruisers** race, with about 250 yachts arriving there in December. There is an annual regatta to coincide with the boats leaving the Canary Islands in November. **Soufrière** has a good anchorage, but as the water is deep it is necessary to anchor close in. There is a pier for short term tie-ups.

Boat trips down the west coast of the island usually include transport, lunch, drinks and snorkelling gear.

Destination St Lucia (DSL), *Rodney Bay Marina, T758-452 8531, www.dsl-yachting. com*. Bareboat or skippered yacht charters, multilingual staff.

Endless Summer, *T758-450 8651, www. stluciaboattours.com*. Catamaran sunset cruises from The Landings marina to Choc Bay and Vigie, US$75 plus 10% VAT including drinks and snacks, or full-day cruises from Rodney Bay marina along the coast to Soufrière, US$110 plus 10% VAT, including tour on land and lunch; private charters including weddings.

St Lucia with children

St Lucia is every kid's dream, with safe Caribbean beaches to play on and plenty to do inland, exploring the rainforest and finding the birds and animals that inhabit the island, or touring a plantation and learning about the colonial way of life, slavery, pirates and brigands. Nowhere is far away so they won't get bored in a car for long, although a supply of travel sickness remedies might be useful for the mountain roads. The lack of museums and buildings of architectural interest means you won't be trailing them around in the heat against their will. The beaches are the main attraction, with lots of watersports on offer for kids of all ages, as well as catamaran trips along the coast to avoid the twisty roads. Many families opt for the all-inclusive resorts to entertain their children, but there are plenty of other ways of providing them with stimulation and enjoyment without confining them to the grounds of one hotel. Teenagers will enjoy Friday nights at the Anse La Raye fish fry or the Gros Islet jump-up where there is music and dancing until you or they drop.

Kids are accepted at most hotels, although some of the Sandals properties are for couples only. At the smaller hotels they are welcomed and many now have self-catering facilities so you can prepare snacks and light meals when they are needed. Food is easy, with lots of places selling burgers, pizzas, pasta or chicken and chips. Most restaurants have international-style menus with local specialities to tempt the adventurous. Life is a little easier if they eat fish.

The Moorings, *Marigot Bay, T758-451 4357, www.moorings.co.uk.* Bareboat and crewed fleet of yachts, also power boats, watersports, diving, windsurfing. Closed Aug-Sep.

Segway
LucianStyle Segway, *11 Reduit Beach Av, T758-724 8200, www.lucianstyle. com.* Mt Pimard Nature Trail Experience US$93.50, Sunset Segway with dinner on the beach, US$108.90, including VAT. Very popular adventure for all the family. You get a bit of training and practice to make sure you can handle your Segway and then you set off on the trail with a guide to point out plants and wildlife and explain the Second World War military history of the area around

Mt Pimard in Rodney Bay. You can see sealed bunkers which were tunnels, storage and lookouts for the US military.

Squash and tennis
Many hotels have tennis courts, some of them lit for night play.
Rex St Lucian Hotel, *Rodney Bay, T758-452 8351, www.rexresorts.com*, has tennis courts for public bookings and lessons as well as for guests.
The St Lucia Racquet Club, *Cap Estate, T758-450 0106.* 9 floodlit tennis courts and squash court with instruction. They host an annual competition open to all amateur tennis and squash players.

Tour operators
Eco South Tours, *Maria Islands Interpretation Centre, Anse de Sables, Vieux Fort*, T758-454 5014, *ecosouthtoursinc@gmail.com*. Formed by the Saint Lucia National Trust to manage and oversee tours within the Pointe Sable Environmental Protection Area (PSEPA), they offer hiking the Mankoté Mangrove Trail, through the protected mangrove forest and along the largest pond in the island, birdwatching along the way; tours of the Maria Islands Nature Reserve; half-day fishing trips with local fishermen on their pirogues, participating in traditional fishing methods; handicraft demonstrations and participating in their production; horse riding along the Mankoté Mangrove trail, Pointe Sable Beach, Bois Chadon and Moule-à-Chique; demonstration of sea moss harvesting at Bois Chadon beach followed by a drink of sea moss.

Heritage Tours, T758-458 1454, *www.heritagetoursstlucia.org*. **Heritage Tours** were developed to give greater community involvement in tourism, with environmental sustainability and economic viability. They offer turtle watching, birdwatching and hiking up La Sorcière or Gros Piton. If you book a tour you can visit a number of different places including **Latille Falls** (20-ft waterfall and pools where you can swim), **Fond d'Or Nature and Historical Park** (hiking trails to plantation house ruins, Amerindian remains and the beach), **Fond Latisab Créole Park** (demonstrations of traditional methods of making cassava bread, etc), **Fond Doux** (19th-century plantation house and nature trails through fruit gardens, where the Battle of Rabot was fought against the British army) and the **Folk Research Centre** (19th-century building

on Mount Pleasant documenting Kwéyòl culture and history). They also run a **Castries Heritage Walk** telling you about the architectural history of the city and an east coast hike with lunch.
St Lucia Reps/Sunlink Tours, T758-452 8232, *www.stluciareps.com*.

Whale watching
Captain Mike's (Mike Hackshaw), T758-452 7044, *www.captmikes.com*. Whale watching as well as sport fishing and pleasure cruises. They use a 60-ft boat, *Free Willy*, which has an upper and lower deck for viewing, and the trip lasts 3 hrs, US$50. Private charters available, taking in beach stops and snorkelling.
Hackshaw's Boat Charters, T758-453 0553. US$60 for a 3-hr trip from Vigie Marina.
Mystic Man Tours, *Soufrière*, T758-459 7783, *www.mysticmantours.com*. 3-hr whale-watching trips with a 2 power boats also used for fishing.

Windsurfing and kiteboarding
The Reef Kite and Surf, *next to The Reef Beach Café, Anse de Sables*, T758-454 3418. See *www.slucia.com/windsurf* and *www.slucia.com/kitesurf*.

Transport

Air
See Getting there, page 131, for details of airports and how to get to St Lucia by air. Check in is 3 hrs before an international flight.

Boat
Ferries around the island include:
Rodney Bay Ferry shuttles between the marina shops, hotels, restaurants, bars and Pigeon Island. The **Gingerbread Express** in Marigot Bay costs EC$5

return, but is refunded by **Doolittle's Restaurant** if you eat or drink there and present your tickets. Water taxis and speedboats can be rented.

Water taxis ply between Soufrière waterfront and **Anse Chastenet**; it's easier than driving the awful road.

Bus

Bus stands in Castries are at the bottom of Darling Rd on the west side of the gardens and extending back to the multi-storey car park on Peynier St. **Route 1** is Castries to **Gros Islet**, **Route 2** Castries to **Vieux Fort**, **Route 3** Castries to **Soufrière**, **Route 4 Vieux Fort environs**, **Route 5 Castries central zone**. Each route then has sub-routes, eg Route 1A is Castries–Gros Islet, Route 1B is Castries–Union–Babonneau, etc.

Car

See also Getting around, page 134. Driving is on the left. Filling stations are open Mon-Sat 0630-2000, some are open later but none is open 24 hrs, selected garages open Sun and holidays 1400-1800. The price of fuel is regularly adjusted by the government for market conditions. Most people ask for how much they want by value rather than in litres, asking for EC$40 or EC$50-worth of fuel. Filling stations do not accept credit cards.

Car hire It is often cheaper to organize car hire from abroad. You can only hire a car if aged 25 or over and have had a licence for 2-3 years; often people over 60 need special authorization from their insurance company or if over 65 a letter from their doctor. The cost is about US$50-100 per day, with discounts for weekly rates. Some car hire companies are open to negotiation.

Optional collision damage waiver is another US$10-22 per day. VAT is added to everything. A St Lucian driver's permit costs US$21/EC$54 for up to 3 months. If arriving at George FL Charles (formerly Vigie) Airport, get your international licence endorsed at the immigration desk (closed 1300-1500) after going through customs. Car hire companies can usually arrange a licence. Check for charges for pick-up and delivery. If dropping off a car at George FL Charles Airport you can sometimes leave the keys with the tourist desk if there is no office for your car hire company.

Motorcycle

Make sure you wear a helmet and have adequate insurance. The roads are dangerous, with blind bends in the mountains and fast traffic, often on the wrong side of the road. Regulations regarding permits and age restrictions are the same as for hiring a car. **Scottie's**, (T758-450 1404, www.stluciascooters. com). Have motorbikes and scooters.

Taxi

Most taxi drivers are well-trained and knowledgeable about their country. They make excellent guides for an island tour, which can work out economical if there are enough of you to fill a car. Some drivers use 14-seater minibuses for larger groups. **North Lime Taxi Association** (Rodney Bay Village, T758-452 8562), the **Soufrière Taxi Association** (Bay St, T758-459 5562, www.soufrieretaxi. com) and the **Southern Taxi Association** (Hewanorra International Airport, Vieux Fort, T758-454 6136, www.southerntaxi. com), all offer taxis, tours and airport transfers, with individual drivers affiliated to their regional association. See page 135.

Martinique
Fort-de-France

Ferries leave Castries Monday, Thursday and Sunday for Roseau with a stop in Fort-de-France. It is well worth considering spending a day or two here: the bars, restaurants, and shops give a French atmosphere quite unlike that of other Caribbean cities.

Fort-de-France was originally built around the Fort St-Louis in the 17th century. The settlement's first name was Fort-Royal and its inhabitants are still called Foyalais. The city of today consists of a crowded centre bordered by the waterfront and sprawling suburbs extending into the surrounding hills and plateaux. Traffic is very dense. Most people live in the suburbs and even the discos are out of the old town centre, which is deserted at weekends after Saturday midday.

The port is to the east of the town centre, where the Baie du Carenage houses the naval base, yacht club, cargo ships and luxury cruise liners.

Fort St-Louis and La Savane

The impressive **Fort St-Louis** still functions as a military base. Built in Vauban style, it dominates the waterfront. The ferry terminal is just east of the massive walls. It is still an active military base and was closed to the public after the 9/11 terrorist attack in New York. Adjacent to the fort is **La Savane**, the old parade ground, a 5-ha park planted with lawn, palms, tamarinds, and other tropical trees and shrubs. The park contains statues of two famous figures: Pierre Belain

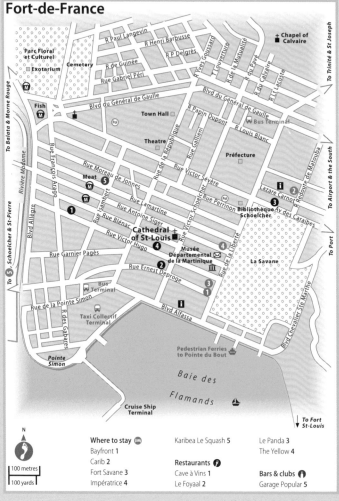

Fort-de-France

Where to stay 🛏
Bayfront 1
Carib 2
Fort Savane 3
Impératrice 4
Karibea Le Squash 5

Restaurants 🍴
Cave à Vins 1
Le Foyaal 2

Le Panda 3
The Yellow 4

Bars & clubs 🍸
Garage Popular 5

d'Esnambuc, the leader of the first French settlers on Martinique, and **Empress Joséphine** (now beheaded by *Independentistes*), first wife of Napoléon Bonaparte, who was born on the island.

Bibliothèque Schoelcher
Corner of rue Victor Sévère and rue de la Liberté, across the road from La Savane, T596-596-702667, Mon 1300-1730, Tue-Fri 0830-1730, Sat 0830-1200.

Schoelcher (1804-1893), who devoted his life to the abolition of slavery, gave much of his library to Martinique, but most was burned in a fire of the town centre in 1890. The building to house the collection was commissioned, but not built, before the fire. It was designed by Henry Picq, a French architect married to a woman from Martinique. The Eiffel engineering company constructed it in iron, shipped it to the island and it opened in 1893. On the exterior you can see the names of freedom campaigners, including John Brown, of the USA, William Wilberforce, of the UK and Toussaint Louverture, of Haiti. Today it still functions as a library and regularly holds exhibitions.

Musée d'Archéologie et de Préhistoire
T596-596-715705, Mon 1300-1700, Tue-Fri 0800-1700, Sat 0900-1700, €1.50.

Just along the rue de la Liberté towards the seafront, this museum contains the best collection in the Caribbean of pre-Columbian relics of the Amerindian tribes: pottery, statuettes, bones, reconstructions of villages, maps, etc.

Cathedral of St-Louis
In the centre of town, in the Square of Seigneur Romero, rue Schoelcher, there is a second chance to see the architecture of Henri Picq with the cathedral, which towers above the Fort-de-France skyline. This, too, is mainly of iron, in a romanesque-byzantine style. The arms of past bishops, in stained glass, give colour to the choir.

Musée Régional d'Histoire et d'Ethnographie de la Martinique
10 Blvd Générale de Gaulle, opposite Atrium Theatre, T596-596-728187, Mon, Wed-Fri 0830-1700, Tue 1400-1700, Sat 0830-1230, €6 for adults, €1 for children and students.

In a beautiful Créole villa dating back to 1887, this modern museum is strong on the origins, customs and traditions of the people of Martinique.

Parc Floral et Culturel
Place José Martí, T596-596-713396, Mon-Thu 0900-1600, Fri 0900-1200, €1.75 adults, €0.50 children.

The Parc Floral et Culturel (which includes the **Galerie de Géologie et de Botanie** and the **Exotarium** aquarium) is a shady park containing two galleries, one of which concentrates on the geology of the island, the other on the flora, and mid-19th-century wooden barracks now housing workshops for local artisans. Almost

2800 species of plants have been identified in Martinique and the Parc Floral has a very good selection.

Markets

Next to the Parc Floral are a feature of Fort-de-France not to be missed: the markets. The **fish market** is by the Madame River, facing the Place José Martí, where fishermen unload from their small boats or *gommiers*. Close by, on rue Isambert, is **Le Grand Marché**, the third of Henri Picq's metal creations (1901) and one of several markets selling fruit, vegetables and flowers as well as exotic spices. The markets hum with activity from 0500 to sunset, but are best on Friday and Saturday.

Listings Fort-de-France

Where to stay

It is difficult to find anywhere to stay for less than about €75 in the city. Cheaper rooms can be found in the suburbs or further afield, but astronomical taxi fares from the ferry terminal make them uneconomical. If you are only staying a night or 2 it is best to get a room in the city centre, in walking distance of the ferry and of all the sights, restaurants, shops and bars for entertainment.

$$$$-$$$ Fort Savane
5 rue de la Liberté, T596-596-807575.
New, smart, modern and comfortable, designed for business and leisure travellers with the perfect location in walking distance of all transport and places of interest. Staff are friendly and helpful, some speak English. Rooms, studios and suites all have queen sized beds, quiet a/c, desks, minibar fridge, espresso coffee machine, Wi-Fi, TV and safe box. Kitchenettes in the studios and suites. Right in the centre of things but double windows overlooking La Savane keep out any noise.

$$$$-$$$ Impératrice
15 rue de la Liberté, T596-596-630682, www.limperatricehotel.fr.
Overlooking La Savane, in the town centre and convenient for the ferry, shops and restaurants, this is one of the best options. Decor and architecture apparently unchanged since it was built in 1957. Largest rooms have view over harbour, smallest rooms look on to inner courtyard. Restaurant and terrace café.

$$$ Bayfront
3 rue de la Liberté, T596-596-555555, bayfronthotel@yahoo.fr.
Overlooking La Savane and the waterfront and in walking distance of the ferry, rooms a good size, simply-furnished, can be noisy if anything is happening at night in that area, tight security, you have to ring the bell to leave or enter. Café/bar/patisserie on ground floor.

$$$ Carib
9 rue Redoute du Matouba, T596-596-601985, www.carib-hotel.com.
16 simple rooms renovated and modernized in 2013. Private showers, a/c, safety box, fridge, free Wi-Fi and good location. No breakfast.

$$$ Karibea Le Squash Hotel
*3 Blvd de la Marne, T596-596-728080,
www.karibea.com.*
105 modern rooms in 2 buildings with
sea view, pool, conference facilities,
impersonal, concrete ambience, rooms
and bathrooms a bit shabby but
breakfast is good. A 20-min walk uphill
from town centre, so best to get a taxi
on arrival.

Restaurants

See also page 26. Good snackbars
and cafés serve various substantial
sandwiches and *menus du jour*. In the
market, upstairs, overlooking shoppers,
are small kiosks selling Créole *menu
du jour*, other meals also served, with
tablecloths and flowers on table, **Chez
Carole** and **Chez Geneviève** are the best
with rum punch (bottle on the table,
self-service), starter, main course, wine
or beer, dessert or coffee for around €15.
As in France, there are *traiteurs* opening
up, offering stylish takeaway meals
which you select at the shop, helpful to
vegetarians. Ask for the latest list at the
tourist office. The place to head for in
the evening when these eateries close, is
the **Blvd Chevalier de Ste-Marthe** next
to La Savane. Here, every evening until
late, vans and caravans serve delicious
meals to take away, or to eat at tables
under canvas awnings accompanied by
loud zouk music. The scene is bustling
and lively, in contrast to the rest of the
city at night-time and the air is filled with
wonderful aromas. Try *lambis* (conch)
in a sandwich or on a *brochette* (like a
kebab) with rice and salad. Paella and
Colombo are good buys and the crêpes
whether sweet or savoury are delicious.

$$$ Cave à Vins
*124 rue Victor Hugo, T596-596-703302,
lacaveavins@wanadoo.fr. Tue-Sat
1215-1400, 1930-2200.*
Smart with white table linen, traditional
French (duck, lamb, terrines, rillettes)
with a local twist, combining ingredients
such as foie gras with fried banana.
Extensive wine list as the name suggests,
but also malt whiskies.

$$$ Le Foyaal
*On the corner of rues Desproges
and Schoelcher, T596-596-630038.
Open 0700-0130.*
On the waterfront, downstairs,
separated from the sea by a car park. A
busy and popular brasserie with indoor
and outdoor tables, lime green, modern
décor, always full at lunchtime, serving
salads and sandwiches as well as full
meals. Service can be haphazard.

$$$ The Yellow
*51 rue Victor Hugo, 1st floor, T596-596-
750359, see Facebook. Open for lunch
and dinner until late.*
The decor is yellow, as you'd expect,
and this modern restaurant is smart but
comfortable. The seafood is fresh and
excellent, the tuna is particularly good,
also the scallops, while the meat is well-
prepared and nicely presented. There is
a set lunch menu and monthly special
theme nights. Tasty cocktails.

$$$-$$ Le Panda
*62 Av de Caraïbes, T596-596-030821,
see Facebook. Open 0600-1630.*
A great café for breakfast, lunch or
just a coffee and snack while you use
the Wi-Fi. Good juices and wonderful
bruschetta with different toppings, see
Facebook for daily menu.

Bars and clubs

Check the local newspaper, France-Antilles, for what's on. There are several bars (*piano bar* or *café théâtre*) where you can listen to various types of music, some have karaoke or cabaret some nights. In Fort-de-France, the best place to find nightlife is the **Blvd Allègre** on the bank of the Madame river, where there are lots of places to choose for late-night music and dancing.

Garage Popular
121 rue Lamartine, T596-596-798676, see Facebook, 1730-0100.
Small bar with tables on the street outside, French and German management, great atmosphere, always lively with different events. Good drinks and cocktails, reasonably priced.

Festivals

Feb/Mar The main pre-lenten **carnival** attracts the whole of Martinique to take to the streets in fantastic costume. Sun is the day of disguises and masked revellers, Mon sees burlesque marriages of improbable couples, Tue **Mardi Gras** is the day of the horned red devils and themed floats. On **Ash Wed**, black and white clad 'devils' parade the streets of Fort-de-France lamenting loudly over the death of Vaval, a gigantic *bwabwa* (the figures carried in *Carnaval*), both the symbol and the presiding 'god' of carnival, his guise differs from year to year. It is chosen secretly by the carnival committee and only revealed at the first parade on Tue.
Apr **Martinique Food Show**, a culinary fair with lots of competitions.
Jul **SERMAC** (Parc Floral et Culturel and at the Théâtre Municipal) organizes a 2-week **arts festival** in Fort-de-France with local and foreign artistes performing plays and dance, T0596-716625.

Dominica

Known as the 'Nature Island' of the Caribbean, Dominica (pronounced Domineeca) is the place to come for dense forests, volcanic hills, rivers, waterfalls and the Boiling Lake. Dominica was the first country to be Green Globe benchmarked. It is also a highly regarded diving destination, with a good marine park system, and for much of the year you can see whales and dolphins offshore. The island is mountainous with very little flat terrain; most settlements hug the coast, usually where the very many rivers – 365 in total – reach the sea. Hotels around the island are small, intimate and low-key, greater development being deterred by the lack of beaches and direct long-haul flights. It is the only island where Caribs have survived and they still retain many of their traditions such as canoe carving. The island's culture and language are an amalgam of the native and immigrant peoples: Carib, French, English and African.

Best for
Canyoning ▪ Diving ▪ Whale watching

Roseau, the capital and main town (population: 20,000), squeezed on a small area of flat land between the sea and the mountains, is small, ramshackle and friendly, with a surprising number of pretty old buildings still intact. The houses look a bit tatty with rusting tin roofs and a general lack of paint through weather damage, but there is still some attractive gingerbread fretwork in the traditional style on Castle Street and others.

A typical house, called a Ti Caz, has a stone base, the walls are boarded with timber and the windows have hurricane shutters for protection or jalousie shutters for privacy. The roofs are steeply pitched, with the ends hipped, giving additional bracing against hurricanes, while verandas give shelter from the sun and rain. Quite a lot of redevelopment has taken place over the last few years, improving access and making the waterfront more attractive.

The centre of Roseau is small enough to walk around, but to get to outlying districts you can catch a bus (minivan) or call a cab. There are lots of car hire companies if you want to drive yourself.

Essential Dominica

Finding your feet

The international airport is in the northeast of the island; take a private or shared taxi to your accommodation, or a bus transfer to the capital. If you are arriving in on the Express des Iles international ferry, the terminal is in central Roseau and an easy walk into town. Buses or taxis will take you from here all over the island.

Diving

If you are coming to Dominica for the diving, dives are usually scheduled early enough in the morning for you to do an onland activity in the afternoon. For your rest day before flying home, plan to do a long hike, such as to the Boiling Lake, which takes most of the day.

Weather Roseau

January	February	March	April	May	June
29°C 22°C 95mm	29°C 22°C 69mm	30°C 22°C 60mm	30°C 23°C 74mm	31°C 24°C 88mm	31°C 25°C 131mm

July	August	September	October	November	December
31°C 24°C 171mm	31°C 24°C 219mm	32°C 24°C 200mm	31°C 23°C 250mm	30°C 23°C 222mm	30°C 22°C 138mm

Dominica

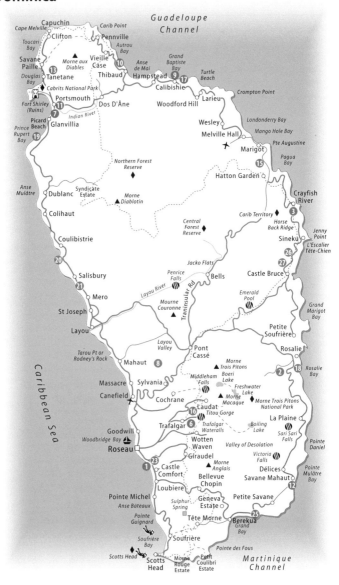

N

| 2 km |
| 2 miles |

Where to stay 🏠

Best places to stay

Cocoa Cottages, page 102
Secret Bay, page 103
Beau Rive, page 105
Jungle Bay, page 105
Pagua Bay House, page 105
Rosalie Bay, page 105

Best activities

Canyoning, page 111
Diving, page 113
Hiking, page 113
Turtle watching, page 114
Whale watching, page 114

Fact file

Location The most northerly of the Windward Islands chain lying between the Atlantic Ocean and the Caribbean Sea, with Guadeloupe to the north and Martinique to the south.
Capital Roseau, 15° 25' 0" N, 60° 59' 0" W
Time zone Atlantic standard time. GMT -4hrs, EST +1hr
Telephone country code +767
Currency East Caribbean dollar, EC$

Old Market area and waterfront

The **Old Market Plaza** is a pedestrian area, with vendors of crafts and souvenirs in the middle. The old, red market cross has been retained, with 'keep the pavement dry' picked out in white paint. Between the plaza and the sea is the old post office, now housing the **Dominican Museum** ① *Bayfront, T767-448 2401, Mon-Fri 0900-1600, Sat 0900-1200, EC$3*, which is well worth a visit. It contains a small display of the geological origins of the island, the first inhabitants, colonization, slavery and emancipation.

The **market**, at the north end of Bay Street, is a fascinating sight on Saturday mornings from about 0600-1000; it is also lively on Friday morning, closed

Roseau

100 metres
100 yards

Where to stay 🛏
Fort Young **1**
La Flamboyant **2**
Ma Bass Central
Guest House **3**
Sutton Place **4**

Restaurants 🍴
Coco Rico Café **1**
Guiyave **2**
Le Bistro **3**
Marvo's Corner **4**
Old Stone Grill
& Bar **5**
Pearl's Cuisine **6**

Tao Restaurant
& Lounge Bar **7**

Buses 🚌
Northbound Buses **1**
Southbound Buses **2**
Buses to Trafalgar &
Laudat **3**

Sunday. The sea wall was completed in late 1993, which has greatly improved the waterfront area of town, known as the **Bay Front** or **Dame Eugenia Charles Blvd**, after the Prime Minister who promoted the development. A promenade with trees and benches, a road from the Old Jetty to Victoria Street, and parking bays take up most of the space. The cruise ship jetty is T-shaped and for a several weeks in the winter season ships tower above the town pouring forth tourists. The ferry terminal is also here.

Botanical Gardens

The 40-acre botanical gardens, founded as an offshoot for Kew Gardens in London and dating from 1891 are principally an arboretum; they have a collection of plant species, including an orchid house. Storms and hurricanes over the last century have taken their toll on the gardens and wiped out the ornamental garden area. You can still see the old bus crushed by a baobab tree during hurricane David in 1979. If you climb the 35 steps of **Jack's Walk** you will get a panoramic view over Roseau, the harbour and the sea. Several Jacquot and Sisserou parrots can be seen in the bird sanctuary in the park, thanks in part to the Jersey Wildlife Preservation Trust. Breeding programmes are underway; some of the offspring will be released to the wild. The gardens are now the main open space and recreational area for Roseau. The Forestry Department's Wildlife Division has a base here.

Windsor Park

The national sports stadium was built as a gift from the People's Republic of China to the standards of the International Cricket Council (ICC) and opened in 2007. It is used for international Test cricket and football matches, but is also the venue for the annual **World Créole Music Festival**. On the site of a former rubbish dump called Cow Town, it was levelled some years ago and used for sporting and entertainment activities before the stadium was built when diplomatic relations were established with China.

Trafalgar Falls

Dominica's most visited site; photogenic and deservedly popular

The Trafalgar waterfalls in the Roseau Valley, 8 km from the capital, have been the most popular tourist site for many years. Hot and cold water flow in two spectacular cascades in the forest, although a hydroelectric scheme higher up and a landslide after the September 1995 hurricanes mean the falls don't have as much water, nor is there such easy access to the pools as a few decades ago. However, if there has been rain, there is too much water to bathe.

The path from the visitor centre to the **viewing platform** at the falls is easy to follow, but if you want to go further than the viewing point, there is a lot of scrambling over rocks and it can be difficult at times. Trying to cross over the falls at the top is very hazardous. Bathing is possible in pools in the river beneath the falls. There are always lots of guides, who can be helpful in negotiating the rough

ON THE ROAD

User fees and site passes throughout Dominica

In theory user fees are required for visits to the following sites maintained by the Forestry, Wildlife and Parks Division (T767-266 3271, http://agriculture.gov. dm/index.php/division/division-of-forestry), although there may not always be someone there to check or punch your ticket. If you are on an organized tour, the operator will have arranged payment in advance and you will not be aware of the fee.

Emerald Pool	Boeri Lake
Cabrits National Park and Fort Shirley	Indian River
Trafalgar Falls	Boiling Lake
Syndicate Forest	Morne Diablotin Trail
Middleham Falls	Freshwater Lake
Soufrière Sulphur Springs	Morne Trois Pitons Trail

Site passes cost US$5 per site or US$12 for a week pass and unlimited visits. These do not include access to the Soufrière/Scotts Head Marine Reserve (SSMR), for which a fee of US$2 is charged per recreational dive, collected by your dive shop.

terrain and boulders for the less mobile visitor. Agree the price before setting out. The Trafalgar Falls are crowded because they are close to the road (bus from outside the Astaphan supermarket in Roseau or walk) and on all the cruise ship excursion itineraries. A natural sulphur pool has been set up at **Papillote** hotel and restaurant by the falls, in lovely gardens.

There is also a road from the sulphur springs of the settlement of **Wotten Waven** through forest and banana plantations across the Trois Pitons River up to the Trafalgar Falls. Screw's Sulphur Spa at Wotten Waven is worth a visit for a bathe in the orange **sulphur pools** ⓘ T767-440 4478, www.scresspa.com, Tue-Sun 1000-2200, Mon if it's a national holiday, US$20, where there are hot, warm and cold pools, you can also have a mud wrap and you get a plate of fruit after your bathe.

Morne Trois Pitons National Park
Dominica's volcanic interior; great scenery and views across the island

The Morne Trois Pitons National Park makes up much of the south part of the island (17,000 acres) and is a UNESCO World Heritage Site. Evidence of volcanic activity is manifested in hot springs, sulphur emissions and the occasional small eruption.

★Boiling Lake
For a description of the hike, see www.avirtualdominica.com/thelake.cfm.

One of the park's main attractions is the Boiling Lake (92°C), which may be the largest of its kind in the world (the other contender is in New Zealand). It is actually a boiling fumarole. Rainwater and a couple of streams flow through the clay and pumice around the lake to hot lava below, where it is heated to boiling point. The grey-blue, bubbling water is enveloped in a cloud of vapour as though in a massive cauldron.

The lake is reached after an eight-mile, three-hour climb from Laudat, returning on the same path. This is probably Dominica's most challenging trail, but also one of the most rewarding and spectacular as you progress through different ecosystems, rising ever higher above the rest of the island with tremendous views. An experienced guide is recommended as, although easy to follow, the trail can be treacherous, particularly when mist descends. They can be found in Laudat. Expect to pay US$60 per person, although this can be negotiated down depending on the size of the group. Make sure you wear clothes you don't mind getting wet and muddy and wear good hiking boots or trainers. The trail is wet and slippery in places and can be as treacherous coming down as going up because of all the steps. Hiking poles can be helpful to reduce stress on your knees. Bring drinks and snacks for energy.

Hikers usually start early in the morning, stop for a break at **Breakfast River**, continue to the **Valley of Desolation** (see below) for a look around and another break, then carry on to the Boiling Lake for a lunch stop. On the return, a drink and a bathe in the **Titou Gorge** is popular to relax the aching muscles. You will be exhausted the next day, so plan for a rest day.

★ Valley of Desolation and Titou Gorge
Below the Boiling Lake is a spectacular region known as the Valley of Desolation, where the forest has been destroyed by sulphuric emissions. At the beginning of the trail to the Boiling Lake is the Titou Gorge, now considerably damaged by rock fall from the hydroelectric development in the area, where a hot and a cold stream mingle. However, there is nothing more refreshing or soothing after hiking to and from the Boiling Lake than swimming through the Titou Gorge.

Kent Gilbert Trail
The Kent Gilbert Trail starts in La Plaine and is about 4½ miles long. It affords views of the Sari Sari and Bolive Falls, but avoids the Valley of Desolation. While this makes it a less strenuous route, it is also less impressive.

Freshwater Lake and Boeri
The **Freshwater Lake**, east of **Morne Macaque** (2500 ft) and two miles from Laudat, can be reached by car passing the highest point you can take a car, at 2789 ft. The road continues from Freshwater Lake to the start of the 25- to 45-minute trail to the island's highest lake, **Boeri**, between Morne Macaque and **Morne Trois Pitons** (4403 ft). The Freshwater Lake is very windy. There used to be kayaking here, but there are currently no activities and it is quiet.

Middleham Trails
The National Park Service has built a series of paths, the Middleham Trails, through the rainforest on the northwest border of the park. The trails are accessible from

Sylvania on the Transinsular Road, or Cochrane, although the signs from Sylvania are not clear.

The road to Cochrane is by the **Old Mill Cultural Centre** in Canefield; once through the village the trail is marked. About 1½ to two hours' walk from Cochrane are the **Middleham Falls** (about 250 ft high) cascading into a very cold but beautiful blue pool in the middle of the forest. The trail is well marked and not particularly strenuous, but a guide can be helpful if you want to know more about what you are seeing and if your party includes anyone who might need help over roots and boulders, such as small children.

Once past the Middleham Falls the trail emerges onto the Laudat road. Turn inland and then immediately right behind the Texaco garage (30 minutes' walk from Roseau) a steep road leads 2½ miles up to **Giraudel** (50 minutes' walk). From behind the school here a trail goes up through a succession of smallholdings to **Morne Anglais** (3683 ft; a two-hour walk from Giraudel). This is the easiest of the high mountains to climb. The trail is fairly easy to follow but someone will need to show you the first part through the smallholdings. Ask in the village or go with a guide.

South coast
a quiet corner of the island with fishing villages and great dive sites offshore

★Soufrière and Scotts Head
In the far south are the villages of **Soufrière** and **Scotts Head**, with a wonderful marine reserve offshore. Both are worth visiting for their stunning setting on the sea with the mountain backdrop and brightly painted fishing boats on the shore. There are plenty of buses to Scott's Head, over the mountain with excellent views all the way to Martinique. Ask around the fishing huts if you are hungry, and you will be directed to various buildings without signs where you can eat a cheap lunch of chicken pilau and watch dominoes being played.

Grand Bay and the Geneva Estate
On the south coast is **Grand Bay**, where there is a large beach (dangerous for swimming) and the 10-ft-high **Belle Croix**. The first settlers in the area were led by a French free black Catholic, Jeannot Rolle in 1691, who came into conflict with the local Kalinago. He had the stone cross built on the coast, expelled the natives and invited the Jesuits to set up a mission. In 1747 the Jesuits founded the island's first Catholic parish in Grand Bay and subsequently set up a plantation, but it was not until the British formally colonized Dominica that the **Geneva Estate** was founded inland, north of the Jesuit estate.

Eighteenth-century plantation agriculture required the importation of large numbers of African slaves, many of whom escaped to the mountains and became maroons. Grand Bay has a reputation for violent resistance. There was a slave revolt in 1791, riots in 1844 and further upheaval in the 1970s over land. The Geneva Estate Great House, at one time the home of the novelist Jean Rhys, was burned

ON THE ROAD

To beach or not to beach

The Caribbean side of Dominica gains or loses sand according to swells and storms but the black coral sandy areas are few and far between. A small one exists just off Scott's Head (favoured as a teaching ground for divers, snorkellers and canoeists, so sometimes crowded), but further north you must travel to Mero Beach or Castaways Beach. Macoucheri Bay and Coconut Beach near Portsmouth are probably the best areas for Caribbean bathing. For some really beautiful, unspoilt white sandy beaches, hire a 4WD and investigate the bays of the northeast coast. Turtle Beach, Pointe Baptiste (impressive red cliffs), Hampstead and Woodford Hill are all beautiful but the Atlantic coast is dangerous. Look at the sea and swim in the rivers is the safest advice. Very strong swimmers may be exhilarated by Titou Gorge, near Laudat, where the water flows powerfully through a narrow canyon and emerges by a hot mineral cascade. Several beaches, coves and rivers were used as locations for the filming of *Pirates of the Caribbean 2* and *3*; tours are available to some sites.

down by arsonists in 1974, but the area is now being developed as a Heritage Tourism Project called the Geneva Heritage Park. Community members have been trained in archaeological methods to identify and preserve key components of their cultural heritage. The estate used to grow and manufacture sugar, bay oil, limes, coconuts, cacao, citrus and vanilla and you can see the methods used. The Grand Bay Arts and Crafts Centre in the Geneva Heritage Park houses locally created arts and crafts, while Coal Pot Soaps is a small cottage industry offering natural, handmade and locally grown herbal products using pure essential oils. From Grand Bay, it is a two-hour walk over the hill, past Sulphur Spring to Soufrière.

Leeward coast
the harbour town of Portsmouth is home to the major historical site of Fort Shirley

North of Roseau

The Leeward coastal road, north from Roseau, comes first to **Canefield**, passing the turning for the twisting Imperial Road to the centre of the island, and then the small airport. The coast road passes through **Massacre**, reputed to be the settlement where 80 Caribs were killed by British troops in 1674. Among those who died was Indian Warner, Deputy Governor of Dominica, illegitimate son of Sir Thomas Warner (Governor of St Kitts) and half-brother of the commander of the British troops, Colonel Philip Warner. From the church perched above the village there are good views of the coast. The next village is **Mahaut** and just north of here Warner Road, climbs steeply up towards Morne Couroune. It then levels out and joins the main Layou Valley road at the Layou Valley Plaza, a few miles west of the Pont Cassé roundabout. The views are stunning and are best when coming downhill.

Central and Northern forest reserves

North of the Transinsular road are the Central Forest Reserve and Northern Forest Reserve. In the latter is **Morne Diablotin** (4747 ft), the island's highest peak. From Dublanc, walk 1½ hours on a minor road and you will see a sign. The trail to the summit is very rough, about three hours' steep walking and climbing up and 2½ hours down, not for the fainthearted. You will need to carry food and water, as there is no stream you can drink from. Wear decent footwear and be prepared for mud. It's best to start early and take a guide.

Portsmouth

The coastal road continues through dry tropical forest typical of this side of the island to Portsmouth, the second town. It is a vibrant place, enlivened by the presence of lots of students from the Ross University campus, who keep the bars and restaurants humming and there is a plentiful supply of good-value accommodation for when their families come to visit. Supermarkets and other food shops are well-stocked with local produce, although you still have to go to Roseau for some imported items. There is a farmers' market on Saturday from 0500.

★ Fort Shirley

At the northern end of Prince Rupert Bay are the remains of the 18th-century Fort Shirley on the **Cabrits National Park** peninsula. The name 'cabrits' comes from the French for the goats which roamed wild on the island before it was joined to the mainland by a causeway.

Unlike Pigeon Island on St Lucia, Fort Shirley has been beautifully restored and the location is scenic enough for weddings to be held here, with a bar and dining room in the former officers' quarters. There is a **museum**, and an excellent plan of how the fort once was. The fort was one of the most important military sites in the West Indies, once housing 600 men to protect the north of the island, and there are gun batteries, store houses and officers' quarters. Clearly marked paths lead to the **Commander's Quarters**, **Douglas** Battery and other outlying areas.

The cruise ship jetty below accommodates only small ships of the Windjammer type, adding to the scenery when a ship in full sail approaches the historic fort. **Prince Rupert Bay** has been much visited: Columbus landed here in 1504, and in 1535 the Spanish Council of the Indies declared the bay a station for its treasure ships. Sir Francis Drake, Prince Rupert and John Hawkins all traded with the Caribs. Construction of Fort Shirley began in 1774. It was abandoned in 1854 and initial restoration began in 1982.

Indian River
Boat trips US$15-25 per person, 40 mins.

From the bridge just south of Portsmouth, boats make regular trips up the river, first through marshland where migrating birds come in the winter and then through a tunnel of vegetation, a peaceful trip as long as you are not accompanied by boatloads of other tourists. Used as a film location for the second *Pirates of*

ON THE ROAD
Pirates of the Caribbean

Whether you've seen the movies or not, the image of Johnny Depp as Captain Jack Sparrow has become synonymous with pirates or, rather, a 21st century romanticized view of pirates. The worldwide runaway success of the first films, shot partly on location in Dominica, put the island on the map for many fans, just as the *Lord of the Rings* brought attention to New Zealand. It did not, unfortunately, prevent some of the film crew's luggage turning up in the Dominican Republic.

In *Dead Man's Chest*, Dominica's northeast coast, with its cliffs and forests, formed the backdrop to many key scenes. Indian River became the 'Pantano River' and was the location for filming boat scenes. The Valley of Desolation became 'Cannibal Island', while 'Shipwreck Cove' was found near Capuchin. Sets were built in Soufrière and Vieille Case, the latter being the site of the ruined church and graveyard on 'Isla Cruces', and the mill from which the giant water wheel breaks free. The runaway wheel rolled to Hampstead Beach where a swordfight between Sparrow, Will Turner (Orlando Bloom) and James Norrington (Jack Davenport) was staged. Other film locations included Pagua Bay, Titou Gorge, where Will Turner and his shipmates were suspended in cages made of bones, High Meadow, where the native village of Pelegostos was built and Pointe Guinade.

Inhabitants still tell tales of the bountiful time when the island was dazzled by the filming and movie stars dined in local restaurants. Taxi drivers are full of stories of who they had in the back of their cab. **Silks Hotel** is proud to show you the rooms where Kiera Knightley and Geoffrey Rush slept, while **Picard Beach Cottages** has named its rooms after the crew members who stayed there. Johnny Depp lived on his private yacht offshore. True fame, however, must be found in the fact that Lego created their two *Pirates of the Caribbean* from Dominican locations: The Mill (Hampstead) and The Church (Vieille Case).

the Caribbean film, the river is tidal and brackish through the Glanvilla Swamp, the second largest on the island, with 50 acres of swamp to the south side. It is a productive fish nursery and you will see lots of crabs eating the algae on the roots of swamp fern and maybe an iguana on a tree overhanging the water. Your boatman should explain what you are seeing and give background information.

There is a bar open at the final landing place on this lovely river which accommodates large numbers of cruise ship passengers and serves them the very potent spiced rum, aptly named *Dynamite*. Alternatively there are local juices and herbal teas. Unfortunately there is very loud music played in the afternoons, but it is quiet in the mornings. Some boatmen offer an early morning tour at about 0700, which is good for seeing birds and very peaceful. When you get up the river as far as you can go, there is a short walk you can take through fruit trees to see what grows here.

North of Portsmouth

From Portsmouth, a road carries on past the Cabrits National Park to the fishing communities of **Douglas Bay** then to the most northerly village of **Capuchin** and the island's north tip at **Cape Melville**. A road leads off this at Savanne Paille; it is a beautiful journey over the mountain, through a valley with sulphur springs, to **Penville** on the north coast, where you can pick up the road heading south.

Calibishie coast

Another road from Portsmouth heads east, following the Indian River for much of the way, winding up and down to the bays and extensive coconut palm plantations of the north coast, Calibishie, Melville Hall Airport and Marigot. There are some beautiful sandy beaches at **Hampstead** (where Dead Man's Chest was filmed) and **Larieu**. While some beaches are protected by rocks and reefs, take advice locally about where to swim as this is the Atlantic coast. There are hiking trails to the forest and wide, sandy beaches nearby; local guides are available. The final sections of the Waitukubili National Trail (see box, page 112) follow the coast all around the north of the island, skirting Morne aux Diables, through Capuchin to the Cabrits National Park. Transport to most areas in the north is good, as is accommodation.

Calibishie is a charming fishing village looking across to Guadeloupe. It is well-served with small shops, post office, petrol station, health clinic, grocery stores and restaurants, and accommodation is mostly self-catering. **Hodges Beach** is one of the nicest beaches in the area and you can swim here. It is protected by a series of small islands and a little reef where you can snorkel. Hodges River comes out to the sea here, a great playground for children and somewhere to wash off salt and sand. **Woodford Hill Beach**, **Turtle Beach** and **Pointe Baptiste Beach** are also within walking distance of Calibishie, all of which are visited by turtles which lay their eggs in the sand in March-May. The leatherbacks come first, followed by the hawksbills, all of them protected by local volunteers.

Transinsular road
Dominica's mountainous interior with rivers and waterfalls for cooling off

The shortest route from Roseau to Marigot and Melville Hall is via the Transinsular Road. It climbs steeply with many bends from Canefield, in the west of the island. You will see coconut and cocoa groves, banana plants all along the gorge, together with dasheen, tannia, oranges and grapefruit. At Pont Cassé, the road divides three ways at one of the island's few roundabouts.

West from Pont Cassé

Heading west from Pont Cassé the road affords some spectacular views. **Layou River** has some good spots for bathing, one of which is particularly good. Just over five miles from the roundabout there is a narrow footpath on the right, immediately before a sizeable road bridge. It passes through a banana field to the riverside. On the opposite bank a concrete bath has been built around a hot spring to create an open-air hot tub (Glo Cho) with room for four or five good friends.

North from Pont Cassé

Heading north from Pont Cassé, a 20-minute walk from **Spanny's Bar** on the main road leads you to **Penrice Falls**, two small waterfalls. There is great, but cold, swimming in both pools. At Bells there is a fascinating and beautiful walk to **Jacko Flats**. Here a group of maroons (escaped slaves) led by Jacko had their encampment in the late 17th and early 18th centuries. Carved into the cliffs of the Layou River gorge, a flight of giant steps rises 300 ft up to a plateau where the maroons camped. Ask in Bells village for a guide and dress for river walking since much of the trail is in the river itself.

East from Pont Cassé

Heading east from Pont Cassé, the path up the Trois Pitons is signed on the right just after the roundabout, three hours to the summit. The **Emerald Pool** is a small, but pretty waterfall in a grotto in the forest, 15 minutes by path from the Pont Cassé–Castle Bruce road. Don't go when cruise ships have docked. There is a reception area, with snack bar, interpretation centre, stalls and toilet facilities. There are no buses from Roseau. Catch a minibus to Canefield and wait at the junction for a bus going to Castle Bruce.

Atlantic coast

rugged, windswept coastline with scalloped bays and dramatic cliffs

Castle Bruce and the Carib Territory

Castle Bruce is a lovely bay and there are good views all around. After Castle Bruce the road enters the **Carib Territory**, although there is only a very small sign to indicate this; to appreciate it fully; a guide is essential. Over 2000 descendants of the original inhabitants of the Caribbean, the once warlike Caribs, live in the Carib Territory, a 3700-acre 'reservation' established in 1903. There are no surviving speakers of the Carib language on the island.

Horseback Ridge affords views of the sea, mountains, the Concord Valley and Bataka village. At **Crayfish River**, a waterfall tumbles directly into the sea by a beach of large stones. Nearby is the **Carib Model Village**, or **Kalinago Barana Autê** ⓘ *T767-445 7979, www.kalinagobaranaaute.com, US$10 site pass; tours, drinks, meals and performances cost extra*. The Kalinago (Carib) people have a reception centre, snack bar and gift shop with an easy trail round the huts (*ajoupas*) in the village. A Karbet (the biggest hut) is used for cultural and theatrical performances. Traditional activities include canoe building, cassava processing, calabash decorating, basket weaving and cooking, although only basket weaving is demonstrated here. You can buy pottery, woven goods, coconut products and other crafts. There are also craft stalls along the road where you can stop if you don't like the pressure to buy here. The basket work is beautiful and very skillful.

The **Save the Children Fund** assisted the Waitikubuli Karifuna Development Committee to construct two traditional buildings near **Salybia**: a large oval *karbet* (the nucleus of the extended Carib family group), and an A-frame *mouina*. The former is a community centre, the latter a library and office of the elected chief. The Carib chief is elected for five years and his main tasks are to organize the distribution of land and the preservation of Carib culture. The Church of the Immaculate Conception at Salybia is based on the traditional *mouina* and has a canoe for its altar, murals about Carib history both inside and out. Outside is a cemetery and a three-stone monument to the first three Carib chiefs after colonization: Jolly John, Auguiste and Corriett.

L'Escalier Tête-Chien, at Jenny Point in Sineku, is a line of rocks climbing out of the sea and up the headland. It is most obvious in the sea and shore, but on the point each rock bears the imprint of a scale, circle or line, like the markings on a snake. It is said that the Caribs used to follow the snake staircase (which was made by the Master Tête-Chien) up to its head in the mountains, thus gaining special powers. Do not go without a guide.

South of Castle Bruce

If, instead of taking the road past the Emerald Falls to Castle Bruce, you take the right fork, you get to the Atlantic coast at **Rosalie Bay**. A black-sand beach extends south from the mouth of the river and is a favoured nesting site for green, hawksbill and leatherback turtles. There is a turtle watch programme on the beach in front of the **Rosalie Bay Resort**. The owner, Beverley Deikel, set up the Rosalie Sea Turtle Initiative (RoSTI) when she discovered the turtles nesting on the property and, by involving local people and guests in the protection programme, succeeded in raising the number of nests from seven leatherback nests in 2003 to 69 nests of all three species by 2010, with 100% survival rate. The initiative has now been expanded throughout Dominica, winning accolades and awards for its work. Together, RoSTI and the Dominica Sea Turtle Conservation Organization (DomSeTCO) run a coordinated, community-based, ecotourism and management programme for sea turtles. In 2015, they were faced with the problem (common to most Caribbean islands) of huge amounts of sargassum seaweed being washed up on Atlantic beaches, including Rosalie Bay, and consequently low levels of turtles arriving to nest on their usual beaches. Climate change, which warms the oceans and slows currents, helps the reproduction of the seaweed bringing monster sargassum blooms. Beaches were several feet deep in rotting weed, which was laboriously cleared and used for iron-rich compost. The turtles went elsewhere or dropped their eggs at sea.

In the southeast at La Plaine a fairly easy trail can be followed to the **Sari Sari Falls** (about 150 ft high), although it involves river hiking and a certain amount of scrambling over boulders. At Délices, you can see the **Victoria Falls** from the road. Take an experienced guide (ask around in the villages, but they will probably find you) if you want to attempt the steep hike to either of these falls and avoid them in the rainy season. The White River falls in to the Atlantic at **Pointe Mulattre**, reached by a steep road from Delices down to the sea. There are great places to picnic, rest or swim in the river. At the weekend local families picnic and wash their cars here. Be wary of flash floods and do not cross the river after heavy rainfall.

The road between **Petite Savanne** and the **White River** links the south and east coasts. It is extremely steep but offers spectacular views of both the Victoria Falls and the steam rising from the Boiling Lake.

Listings Dominica

Tourist information

Discover Dominica Authority
Roseau on 1st Floor, Financial Centre, Kennedy Av, T767-448 2045, www.dominica.dm.
There are information offices at Melville Hall airport, Canefield airport and Bayfront, by the cruise ship terminal.

Tip...

See the website **www.dominica.dm** for useful information.

Where to stay

Roseau *p87, map p90*
There are some small, informal hotels and guesthouses not listed here. Do verify whether VAT (10%) and service (10%) are included in the quoted rate. Apartments are available to rent in and around Roseau; check at the tourist office, look in the weekly *Chronicle* or ask a taxi driver.

$$$$-$$$ Fort Young Hotel
Within the old fort, T767-448 5000, www.fortyoung hotel.com.
Ocean front and inland view, standard and deluxe rooms and suites of fine standard and full conference facilities for the business traveller, lots of facilities, tour desk, dive shop linked to **Dive Dominica**, small spa, food adequate, pool, exercise room, jetty, waterfront restaurant, relaxed atmosphere at weekends, special events like concerts and barbecues, live band at **Boardwalk Bar** on Fri night. Good rum punch and happy hour. The bar is popular during the day with cruise ship passengers as it is very close to the jetty and the town centre.

$$$ Sutton Place Hotel
25 Old St, T767-449 8700, www.suttonplacehoteldominica.com.
Rooms and self-catering suites, facilities for business travellers, central and convenient, bar and restaurant open daily, **Pearl's Cuisine** on site for lunch and dinner.

$$$-$$ La Flamboyant
22 King George V St, T767-440 7190, www.laflamboyanthotel.dm.
Multicoloured exterior, modern design, rooms with fridge, some have a/c, avoid rooms overlooking noisy karaoke bar, convenient for town centre and ferry.

$$ Ma Bass Central Guest House
44 Fields Lane, T767-448 2999,
www.mabassdominica.com.
11 rooms on 4-floor house built by
Mr Bass, simple lodging, clean and
friendly, fans or a/c, Mrs Bass will cook
or give you use of kitchen and is full of
useful information.

Trafalgar Falls *p91, map p88*

$$$ Cocoa Cottages
Roseau Valley, T767-295 7272,
www.cocoacottages.com.
Deep in the countryside, rustic charm
and comfort, cottages in lush gardens
with hammocks, verandas and a
back-to-nature feel, very laid back and
relaxing. Breakfast and evening meal at
additional cost, served communal style
around large table, friendly and sociable.
Host Iris is artistic and creative, making
chocolate as well as other skills. Linked
to **Extreme Dominica** for canyoning and
rappelling.

$$$ Papillote Wilderness Retreat
T767-448 2287, www.papillote.dm.
Suites or cottage in beautiful botanical
gardens www.papillotegardens.com,
landscaped by owner Anne Jno Baptiste,
with hot mineral pools and geese,
birdwatching house. The gardens were
demolished by Hurricane David in 1979
but are now one of the most spectacular
in the region, with over 100 genera and
more than 600 individual species. Food
good but slightly limited for long stay,
closed Sun (avoid days when cruise
ship passengers invade, reservations
required), arts and crafts boutique, take
torch and umbrella, good road from the
nearby village of Trafalgar all the way to
the falls car park, spectacular setting.

$$-$ Chez Ophelia Cottage Apartments
Roseau Valley, T767-448 3438,
www.chezophelia.com.
Your host is the famous singer Ophelia,
Dominica's 'First Lady of Song'. 5 simple
cottages, in traditional style, each with
two connecting apartments sleeping
4 in small bedroom, bathroom, kitchen
and living room with twin beds. Popular
with families and school groups, meals
by reservation. Good hiking in the area,
close to Wotten Waven Sulphur Springs
or Trafalgar Falls.

South coast *p94, map p88*

$$$$-$$$ Titiwi
Citronier, T767-448 0553,
www.titiwi.com.
Seafront studios and apartments just
south of Roseau, well-equipped, pool,
owners on site for help with anything.

$$$ Anchorage
*On seafront, Castle
Comfort, T767-448 2638,*
www.anchoragehotel.dm.
Long-established dive resort. Waterfront
restaurant, variety of poolside or
oceanfront rooms, nothing fancy, bar,
friendly but slow service, food nothing
special but Thu barbecue buffet with live
music, performance poetry and dancing,
good and popular with locals, swimming
pool and diving facilities, dive packages
available, whale watching.

$$$ Castle Comfort Lodge
*On seafront, Castle Comfort, T767-448
2188, www.castle comfortdivelodge.com.*
Very friendly, professional dive lodge,
14 simple rooms, some nicer than others,
excellent local food, good service. Dive
packages available including transfers,
tax and service.

Leeward coast *p95, map p88*

$$$$ Crescent Moon Cabins
Rivière La Croix, high above Mahaut but reached from the main Transinsular Rd, about 30 mins from Roseau, T767-449 3449, www.crescentmooncabins.com.
Well-furnished wooden cabins in a delightful, secluded setting with magnificent view down to the sea, run by Americans Ron (chef) and Jean Viveralli (Montessori teacher, school attached), good home cooking, fresh organic fruit and vegetables from on-site greenhouse and gardens, own roasted coffee and cocoa, goats and chickens, fresh spring water, water from Riviere La Croix, drinking water from a spring, breakfast included, dinner US$40, car hire recommended, lots of hiking information.

$$$$-$$$ Tamarind Tree Hotel & Restaurant
Near Salisbury, T767-449 7395, www.tamarindtreedominica.com.
On cliff between Macoucherie and Salisbury beaches, halfway between Roseau and Portsmouth, very quiet, Swiss/German-run, simple rooms in hotel or cottages with living/dining/kitchen upstairs opening onto deck with sea view and 2 bedrooms downstairs, fan, pool, restaurant closed Tue except with reservation, meal plans available, Kubuli beer on draught. Closed Sep.

$$$ Sunset Bay Club
Batalie Beach in the middle of the west coast, T767-446 6522, www.sunsetbayclub.com.
Run by French-speaking Belgian family, all-inclusive or bed and breakfast, rooms in concrete bungalows, get one in front row for view, fan, simple furnishings, pool, pebbled beach changes to sand

in the water, discounts for children. Restaurant famous for its lobster. **Sea Side Dive** shop on site.

Portsmouth *p96, map p88*

$$$$ Picard Beach Cottage Resort
T767- 445 5131, www.picardbeachcottages.dm.
Wooden cottages on large black sand beach, many named after the Pirates of the Caribbean crew members who stayed here. Those closest to the sea are slightly bigger with larger kitchens and more expensive than those behind, some of which need renovating. Good sea bathing with coral reef for snorkelling, lovely gardens, fruit trees, iguanas in the trees, yoga, beach bar and restaurant. The rooms furthest away from the bar are the quietest. Student parties on the beach can be noisy; Ross University is close by.

$$$$ Secret Bay
Tibay, T767-445 4444, www.secretbay.dm.
Luxury cottages and villas in small resort on cliff overlooking sea, very secluded and private, fabulous views, great sunset watching from verandas, access to 2 sandy beaches, Tibay and Secret Bay with its cave and rock arches, good snorkelling, kayaks for exploring further afield, Cario River at edge of property, Fully equipped kitchens, fruit and herbs in garden for your own use or have meals served on your deck, all diets accommodated, fresh and tasty, excellent food in glorious location.

$$$$-$$$ The Champs
Blanca Heights, Picard, T767-445 4452, www.thechampsdm.com.
On hillside with view of the bay, run by Hans and Lise, 5 rooms, friendly

and helpful service, good Dominican breakfasts, restaurant and pizzeria and lively bar, fine dining Fri night, gourmet brunch Sat morning, see Facebook for what's on, jacuzzi, Wi-Fi.

$$$$-$$$ Manicou River Eco Resort
Everton Hall Estate, Tanetane, T767-616 8903, www.manicouriver.com.
On a former lime and bay oil producing estate, up steep access road, 4WD needed, timber villa and hexagonal tree houses on hillside using local furniture and minimizing the impact on surroundings. Full kitchens, panoramic views from verandas, hammocks, solar power, rainwater, lots of fresh fruit, home-grown and roasted coffee, restaurant planned. Idyllic.

$$$ Sisters Sea Lodge
Prince Rupert's Bay, T767-445 4501.
Swiss-run, 4 spacious, self-contained studios with kitchenettes in 2 bungalows, insect nets, 2 double beds, outdoor stone showers, set in lovely gardens with lawns running down to the sea. Excellent location in walking distance of supermarket, Ross University and Indian River as well as buses, convenient for hikers of Waitukubuli Trail, yachts can moor in the bay, sandy outside beach bar/restaurant, good food, great rum punch.

The north *p98, map p88*

$$$$ Pointe Baptiste
Calibishie, T767-445 7368, www.pointebaptiste.com.
Pointe Baptiste Estate covers 25 acres of gardens, orchard and forest on the northern tip of the island looking out towards Marie Galante and Les Saintes, with 2 beaches and cove to explore. The Main House sleeps 6-8,

includes cook and maid, weekly rates available, spectacular view from the airy veranda, cool breezes, house built in 1932, wooden, perfect for children, cot, also smaller house sleeping 2 (**$$$**), self-catering, book locally through the manager, Alan Napier.

$$$$-$$$ Calibishie Cove
Calibishie, T767-265 1993, www.calibishiecove.com.
On hilltop with expansive views over the ocean to Marie Galante, 4 spacious and breezy suites, all with sea view on both sides, good kitchens and shower, penthouse has plunge pool, solar power, no restaurant but breakfast can be delivered to your room and other meals also available including local specialities such as curried goat and pumpkin soup, kayaks available.

$$$ Calibishie Lodges
Calibishie, T767- 445 8537, www.calibishie-lodges.com.
Close to all village amenities, on hillside up lots of steps from pool at entrance. Restaurant on terrace overlooking pool, facing inland. Studios are small with kitchenettes but adequately equipped, village atmosphere, great people watching from balcony, friendly. Rooms on top floor more expensive than those below. Also a luxury villa with 4 suites and an apartment to rent.

$$$ Comfort Cottages
Terre Platte, Blenheim, T767-445 3245, www.comfortcottages.com.
On hillside overlooking Atlantic coast, 4 fully furnished and comfortable cottages with plunge pools on veranda, barbecue pit and gazebo in the garden for communal use, bar and restaurant, car hire.

$$$ Sea Cliff Cottages
15 mins' walk from Calibishie, T767-445 8998, www.dominica-cottages.com.
5 cottages above Hodges Bay, 1-2 bedrooms, full kitchens, veranda, fruit and nut trees in the extensive garden for seasonal use, path to beach where turtles nest and swimming is safe because of protection from the reef and islets, snorkelling good, river good for children to play in, small island within swimming distance.

$$$ Veranda View
Calibishie, T445 8900, www.lodgingdominica.com.
Run by multilingual Hermien Kuis, B&B on the beach, beautiful view of Guadeloupe. 2 rooms upstairs share large veranda and sun deck, 1 room downstairs has another veranda. Light cooking facilities, hot showers, breakfast available, other meals by reservation, Hermien is a great cook. Restaurants and other village amenities in walking distance.

$$$ Wind Blow Estate
Calibishie, T767- 445 8198, www.windblowestate.com.
3 apartments, 1 or 2 bedrooms, fans, sun deck, great views across to Guadeloupe, parking, security guard, sisserou parrot nests on the estate.

Atlantic coast *p99, map p88*

$$$$ Beau Rive
Between the Carib Territory and Castle Bruce, T767-445 8992, www.beaurive.com, closed Aug-Sep.
Quiet, elegant, built in the style of a colonial manor house by owner/manager, Mark Steele, and you feel more like house guests than in a hotel. Bright and airy rooms with shower room and balcony, wood floors, simple décor, uncluttered, pool, library, bar always open, buffet breakfast on the terrace included, dinner is a 3-course set menu which changes nightly for about US$40 at 1900. Set in 3 acres of gardens and forest looking down to Anse Français and Wakaman Point, you can walk down the Richmond River to get to the beach, where there is a rock pool you can sometimes bathe in. Note that Mark's friendly dogs and cat live here too. No children under 16.

$$$$ Jungle Bay
White River, Delices, T767-446 1789, www.junglebaydominica.com.
B&B or all-inclusive, luxury cabins on stilts in the forest, rustic elegance, organic food, natural body products, spa, yoga, emphasis on low carbon footprint, lots of steps up to some cabins. Hiking and other activities arranged.

$$$$ Pagua Bay House
Marigot, T767-445 8888, www.paguabayhouse.com.
Stylish and modern, built to look like tin banana-processing sheds. 4 rooms and 2 suites, huge beds with hypoallergenic feather mattresses and pillows, all ocean view, bathrooms with walk-in showers, polished concrete vanities and dark wood floor. Also Pagua Bay Bar & Grill with pool overlooking the ocean.

$$$$ Rosalie Bay
T767-446 1010, www.rosaliebay.com.
Seafront hotel on black-sand beach where turtles nest but you can't swim. Huge, luxury rooms with large bathrooms in pairs of double and twin, all with gorgeous furniture made by Elvis, a local craftsman who used local wood. Wrap-around decks, swing chairs, cathedral ceilings, wheelchair accessible,

spa, business centre, solar power, own water treatment plant, organic garden. Pleasant restaurant at the river mouth.

$$$ Zandoli Inn
Roche Cassée, Stowe, near the fishing village of Fond St Jean in the south, T767-446 3161, www.zandoli.com.
Secluded, superb seaviews across the bay and to Martinique, 5 rooms with balconies, good breakfast, packed lunches available, 4-course dinner at 1900 by reservation, plunge pool, 6 acres of seaside tropical forest, steps down to rocky shoreline.

$$ Carib Territory Guest House
Crayfish River, on the main road, T767-445 7256, www.avirtualdominica.com/ctgh.htm.
Charles Williams (the current Carib chief) and his wife, Margaret, run this guesthouse. She cooks if meals are ordered in advance, good base, he also does island-wide tours but is better on his own patch.

$$ Domcan's Guest House
North of Castle Bruce, T767-445 7794, www.domcans guesthouse.com.
3 new apartments, each with kitchenette, living room, bathroom and bedroom, with one balcony looking inland to the forest and mountains and another looking through the coconut palms to the sea. Domcan's Restaurant attached, where guests get 10% off all meals. On segment 5 of the Waitukubuli Trail.

Camping
Camping in the national parks is forbidden but some places cater for campers.

$$$-$ 3 Rivers Resort
T767-446 1886, www.3riversdominica.com.
On the Rosalie River and in the forest, variety of accommodation, offering cottages, dormitories, tent sites, jungle cabins, hammock space and guided camping tours, award-winning for its green credentials.

Restaurants

In restaurants, 15% VAT is added to meal charges and service charge may also be added.

Roseau *p87, map p90*

$$$ Coco-Rico Café
Bayfront, T767- 449 8686, www.cocoricocafe.com. Mon-Fri 0830-1600, Sat 0830-1400.
Restaurant, bar, gift shop downstairs, excellent range of food from full Créole meals to crêpes, good service, pleasant environment, sidewalk café, indoors with ceiling fans or outside seating under umbrellas. Convenient place to have breakfast while waiting for the inter-island ferry to arrive after you've booked in.

$$$ Guiyave
15 Cork St, T767-448 2930, see Facebook. Mon-Fri 0830-1600, Sat 0830-1400.
For midday snacks and juices, patisserie downstairs and Caribbean lunch buffet from 1130 upstairs, popular, plant-lined balcony, crowded after 1300. Also catering service.

$$$ Le Bistro
19 Castle St, T767-440 8117. Mon-Fri evenings only.
Small bistro with a few tables inside and a few more on a balcony. French and international food with an island twist,

good duck, mussels and steak. Lion fish is on the menu. Ask for the specials.

$$$ Old Stone Grill & Bar
15 Castle St, T767-440 7549.
Good and dependable, fresh and tasty food, friendly if not speedy service, well-stocked bar with good drinks, alcoholic or non-alcoholic.

$$$ Pearl's Cuisine
At Sutton Place Hotel, T767-448 8707.
Good range of inexpensive local food, sit down lunch in dining room, takeaway service at the back, dinner for hotel guests only.

$$$ Tao Restaurant & Lounge Bar
11 Victoria St, T767-316 6666,
see Facebook.
Wide range of styles, Peruvian ceviche or lomo salteado, Mexican burritos, Japanese sushi (Sat nights), sometimes Thai food, or go for a grilled chicken salad. Seafront dining, romantic atmosphere, slow service. Look for special nights, music nights. Art gallery on site.

$ Marvo's Corner
Independence St, T767-225 6247.
Breakfast and mid-morning snacks from roadside snack shop. Créole-style breakfast to takeaway, bakes filled with omelette, codfish, provisions and salad, accras, juices, fruit or vegetable smoothies, and other treats ideal for picnics or hiking food. Also very good is the cocoa tea made with coconut milk, rich and sweet for energy.

Trafalgar Falls *p91, map p88*

$$$ Papillote
See page 102, T767-448 2287.
Daily 0700-2200.
Book before 1600 for an evening meal, take swimming costume and towel to bathe in sulphur pool under the stars.

$$$-$$ Sunshine Cottage
Shawford Estate, T767-285 6399,
www.sunshinecottagedominica.com.
Open Thu-Sat.
Up in the hills above Roseau off the road to Laudat, this is a delightful vegetarian/vegan restaurant serving locally grown organic dishes with a wood-fired pizza oven. Multi-lingual Swiss owner is very hospitable and her husband, the chef, is of Italian ancestry.

South coast *p94, map p88*

$$$-$$ Zam Zam Café
Citronier, next to the Anchorage,
T767-440 7969, see Facebook.
Wed-Sun from 1600.
On the waterfront for great sunset watching. Mexican, quesadillas, nachos, burritos with good cocktails; margarita, tequila sunrise, also mojitos and rum punch. Live music some nights and special barbecue or wine-tasting nights.

Leeward coast *p95, map p88*

$$$-$$ Romance Café
Mero Beach, T767-449 7922,
see Facebook. Breakfast, lunch
and dinner.
Blue and pink building on the beach. Frederica is a welcoming host. You can use the sun beds and spend the day on the beach, showers for customers. Good food, varied menu, French and Créole. Look out for events, such as weekend night time barbecues, the

full moon party with a bonfire and Dominican drummers.

Portsmouth *p96, map p88*
The best restaurants are attached to hotels, eg **Champs** and **Sea Sisters**. On Portsmouth's Bay Rd there are several **snackettes** selling roti and bakes at lunchtime.

$$$ Purple Turtle
Lagon, T767-445 5296. Mon-Fri 1000-2300, Sat-Sun 1000-0200.
Beach bar, snacks and full meals, good roti, local and international food.

$$$-$$ Tomato Café & Deli
Picard, T767-445-3334. Mon-Sat.
Grill nights Mon and Thu. Meats and cheeses flown in from Miami. Canadian-run, North American-style menu with burgers, wraps, wings, paninis, lasagne, brownies and cheesecake. Starbucks coffee and Kubuli beer on tap. Popular with Ross University students.

$ The Shacks
Next to Ross Medical School on the Portsmouth-Roseau road in Portsmouth.
Food stalls serve cheap and good snack food, pizza, hot roti and fried chicken, bakes, pastries, fruit, fresh juices.

The north *p98, map p88*

$$$-$$ POZ Restaurant & Bar at Calibishie Gardens
Main St, Calibishie, T767-445 8327.
Good food, all freshly prepared, allergies and special diets can be accommodated. Local favourites such as goat curry, crayfish and mahi mahi, washed down with some excellent rum punch. Pool available if you want to make a day of it or entertain the children, also tree house rooms for rent if you want to stay over.

$$$-$$ Rainbow Beach Bar
Main St, Calibishie, T767-245 9995, see Facebook.
Fresh, locally sourced, tasty food, all beautifully presented and accompanied by a wonderful seaview. Also rooms available.

Atlantic coast *p99, map p88*

$$$ DomCan's Café
North of Castle Bruce on the main road, T767-445 7754. Open 0900-2200.
Good service, lunch of sandwiches and burgers, dinner fish, chicken.

$$$ Islet View
Castle Bruce, next to DomCan's.
Wonderful view over the bay and Castle Bruce, lovely lunch stop with good local food and extensive selection of infused rums at the bar.

$$$ Pagua Bay Bar & Grill
Marigot, T767-275 9699, www. paguabayhouse.com/BarGrill.aspx. Breakfast and dinner for hotel guests or by reservation only, lunch 1200-1500.
Indoor and outdoor seating overlooking Pagua Bay. Modern, innovative cuisine, food beautifully presented, fresh and tasty. Great place when touring the island.

$$$ Riverside Café
Taberi, La Plaine, T767-446 1234, www. citruscreekplantation.com/rs.html. Open 1000-1700, evenings by reservation only.
French fusion food using local, organic produce and lots of fish and seafood. Beautiful setting beside the Taberi River, where you can bathe while waiting for your food to be cooked.

Bars and clubs

Friday is *the* night out, with people (locals and tourists alike) moving from **Fort Young**'s Happy Hour across to Cellar's Bar at Sutton Place. However, there are a growing number of places to eat and hang out south of Roseau, in the 2-mile stretch from the city centre to the village of Loubiere. They represent a good cross section of bars, places to eat and nightspots, ranging from down-to-earth to upmarket. For lovers of zouk music, look out for live performances by **WCK**, **Midnight Groovers** or **First Serenade**. See *Dominica Events* on Facebook for what's going on.

Cellars Bar
Old St, Roseau, T767-614 3523, see Facebook. Daily 1600-2200, later on Wed and Fri.
Big screen TV, karaoke 1900 every Sat, jazz, a/c.

Fort Young Hotel
Roseau. Mon Caribbean buffet and steel band in the Marquis restaurant, US$32.50, 1830-2200.
Fri after-work lime in the **Balas Bar** in the courtyard, happy hour 1800-2000. Live music until 2230. Popular.

Ruins Rock Café
Between Hanover St and King George V St, T767-4407583, see Facebook.
Excellent rum punches and multi-coloured cocktails, also cold beer. Drinks served in bamboo mugs or coconut shells. Live music.

Spiders
Loubiere, T767-448 4319, see Facebook. Daily 2130-late.
Guaranteed to be open when everywhere else has closed, it is a hole in the wall with great Caribbean music, some of the cheapest beers, fried chicken and the famous *spider pies* (they are actually fish).

Symes-Zee's
King George V St, Roseau, T767-448 2494. Mon-Sat 2200-late.
The spot to be on Thu night with live jazz, nice atmosphere.

Festivals

For information about any festivals contact the **Dominica Festivals Committee** (*T767-448 4833, www.wcmfdominica.com*).

Feb/Mar Carnival is on the Mon and Tue before Ash Wednesday; it lacks the sponsorship of a carnival like Trinidad's, but it is one of the most spontaneous and friendly. Sensay costume has returned to the streets: layer upon layer of banana or cloth is used for the costume, a scary mask is worn over the face, usually with horns, and big platform clog boots finish the effect. Large quantities of beer are required for anyone who can wear this costume and dance the streets for several hours in the midday sun. During Carnival, laws of libel and slander are suspended.

Jun-Jul Fête Marin (St Peter's) in Portsmouth as well as in Soufrière/Scott's Head, Colihaut/Dublanc and Anse de Mai.

Jul Divefest, with lots of activities, races, underwater treasure hunts, cruises, etc. Contact the **Watersports Association** (*T767-448 2188, dive@cwdom.dm*).

Oct Dominica hosts the **World Créole Music Festival**, with Cadence-lypso, Zouk, Compas, Bouyou and Soukous. Artists come from other islands such as Haiti, Martinique and Cuba, or further

ON THE ROAD

Entertainment on Dominica

Dominica is lacking in a well-developed arts scene although performances of plays, concerts, dance shows and recitals are held at the **Arawak House of Culture** in Roseau or sometimes at the **Old Mill Cultural Centre** in Canefield. Friday is the night out, with people moving from one happy hour to another in town, then to bars and finally to clubs along the road south to Loubière, which don't get going until after midnight. There is a thriving music scene. Popular and long-established local bands include **WCK Band**, pioneers of Bouyon music (see Facebook) **First Serenade**, performing since 1984, and **Midnight Groovers**, going strong since 1978, with dozens of albums. **Midnight Groovers** is led by Phillip 'Chubby' Mark, known as the 'King of Cadence-Lypso'. Anthony Gussie leads his band **Black Affairs**, and sings in French, English, Kwéyòl and Kokoy. The **World Créole Music Festival** in October is a great insight into regional music trends, whether it's Cadence, Soukous, Compas, Zouk or Bouyou. Dominica is not all about Créole music, however, and there is plenty of dancehall, reggae and other wider Caribbean styles of music.

afield from Africa, the UK and Louisiana, as well as from Dominica. For where to get single or season tickets for events at Windsor Park Sports Stadium, see www. wcmfdominica.com.

Last Fri in Oct Créole Day, when the vast majority of girls and women wear the national dress, 'la wobe douillette', to work and school and most shop assistants, bank clerks, etc, speak only Créole to the public.

3-4 Nov Independence Day celebrations feature local folk dances, competitions, storytelling, music and crafts.

Entertainment

Theatre
The Arawak House of Culture, *Hillsborough St in Roseau, next to Government HQ, T767-449 1804, see Facebook*. Can seat 540 for plays, concerts, dance shows and recitals.

Old Mill Cultural Centre, *Canefield, T767-449 1804*. Performances are also held here.

Shopping

Roseau *p87, map p90*
Art galleries
The Art Asylum, *Jimmit, Mahaut, T767-449 2484, www.earletienne.com*. The gallery of Earle Etienne, Dominica's best-known artist, teacher and mentor.
Ellingsworth Moses Art Studio & Gallery, *27 King George V St, Roseau, www.emosesart.com*. One of the leading young artists from Dominica working in mixed media. His work can also be seen at Ross University Housing department in Portsmouth, Cocoa Cottages in Shawford, Trafalgar, Coco Rico Restaurant in Roseau, Fort Young Hotel, Everybody's Gallery, and The Old Mill Cultural Centre.

Crafts and gifts

Straw goods are among the best and cheapest in the Caribbean; they can be bought in the Carib Territory and Roseau.

Other good buys are local Bay Rum (aftershave and body rub), coconut soap, tea, coffee, marmalade, hand cream, shampoo, spices, chocolate and candles. Bello 'Special' or 'Classic' pepper sauce is a good souvenir.

Craft Market, *Old Market, Roseau*. A good place to get an idea of what is available.

Food

Brizee's Mart, *5 mins from Roseau centre, T767-448 2087, Canefield. Mon-Thu 0900-2000, Fri-Sat 0900-2100*. One of the largest supermarkets.

Whitchurch Supermarket, *Old St, Roseau. Mon-Thu 0800-1900, Fri-Sat 0800-2000*. Has good range at reasonable prices.

GreenEye Production, *Albert and Julie Joseph in Loubiere at Long Side River Side Cuisine (on the bridge at Grand Bay Junction) or in Roseau at the Sat market, T767-245 4707/315 1066, see Facebook*, use banana, plantain and other provisions such as yam, sweet potato, cocoy and breadnut, all organically grown, non-GMO, sun-dried and gluten-free, to make flour, grain and coffee.

Markets

The farmers' market is held every Fri and Sat morning by the mouth of the Roseau River, very colourful.

Portsmouth *p96, map p88*

Crafts and gifts

Portsmouth has a sizeable craft shop at the Cruise Ship Berth on the Cabrits but prices are much higher than in Roseau.

NDFD Small Business Complex, *9 Great Marlborough St*. Has a wide selection of local crafts.

Food

James Supermarket, *opposite Ross Medical School*. Good selection of staples and imported foodstuffs, frozen meats, ham, etc, also prepaid phone cards.
Whitchurch IGA also has a good selection of packaged goods.

Markets

At Portsmouth and Calibishie there is an excellent farmers' market on Sat from 0500 where you can find fresh fruit, vegetables and spices locally grown. There is also a small market area beside Ross University grounds where you can get fruit, vegetables, yoghurt and prepared meals.

What to do

Adventure parks

Wacky Rollers, *8 Fort St, Roseau, T767-440 4386, www.wackyrollers.com*. Adventure park on the Layou River in the forest with suspended walkways and platforms connected by cables, ziplines and a Tarzan jump. Varied levels for different abilities, a children's park and picnic area. Opening times restricted if it is a non-cruise ship day. There is also river tubing, kayaking tours and jeep tours. They use ex-army vehicles and Land Rovers, all individually painted by Earl Etienne (see Art galleries, above).

Canyoning

See Planning your trip, page 15.
Extreme Dominica, *Roseau Valley, T767-295 7272, www.extremedominica. com*. Canyoning tours take you into breathtaking river canyons where you

ON THE ROAD

★ Waitukubuli National Trail

The Caribs, or Kalinago, who supplanted the Arawaks on Dominica, called the island Waitukubuli ('tall is her body'), and it is this name which has been adopted for the national trail network opened in 2011, www.waitukubulitrail.com. Divided up into 14 manageable sections, the trail runs for 115 miles from the far south at Scotts Head to the north at the Cabrits Peninsula, taking in most of Dominica's attractions: east and west coasts, north and south tips, forests, rivers and mountains. Very much a community tourism project under the aegis of the Forestry Department, old roads have been rehabilitated, whether they were originally slave trails, smugglers' routes, Kalinago paths or donkey tracks, with each village clearing bush and undergrowth, building bridges, steps and handrails on their sections. You can walk just one or two sections or tackle the whole trail, staying at community-run lodgings, such as homestays (Homestay coordinator, T767-449 6853, vidalkforever@msn.com), small B&Bs or camping. Guides are available in the villages if you need one or the Waitukubuli National Trail Management Unit, T767-266 3593, wntp@cwdom.dm, has a list of certified guides, but the trails are well marked and maps are available if you want to do it without. You should fill in a hikers' registration form before setting out and there is lots of help on planning your hike on the website. A day pass to hike one or more segments is US$12, while a 15-day pass to hike all 14 segments is US$40.

rappel down hidden waterfalls and jump into crystal clear pools. No experience necessary and all equipment and training is provided. Bring swimsuit and sneakers/trainers. Go Pro helmet cam rentals available to record your journey. Professional guides trained by the American Canyoning Association. Also hiking tours such as to the Boiling Lake and Secret Beach.

Climbing
Mountain climbing can be organized through the **Forestry Division** (T767-448 2401). Guides are necessary for any forays into the mountains or forests, some areas of which are still uncharted.

Cricket
Cricket is played at the **Botanical Gardens** or at the **Petite Savanne**. The **Windsor Park** national stadium in Roseau is of ICC standard and hosts international Test matches. It is the home of the **Dominica Cricket Association** (T767-440 6519, www.dominicacricketassociation.com). The next best pitch is at **Macoucherie**, close to the rum distillery.

Cycling
There are lots of trails for off-road cycling but, as yet, mountain biking is very small scale. Most people who cycle on the island bring their own bikes with them. Contact the **Dominica Cycling Association** (see Facebook) for more information.

Diving

For dive sites, see Planning your trip, page 16.

Snorkelling trips, around US$30 are particularly recommended for the Champagne area.

Scuba diving is permitted only through one of the island's registered dive operators or with written permission from the **Fisheries Division**. Single-tank dives are from US$55 and 2-tank dives are from US$75. Remember to add equipment rental, marine reserve fee, VAT and credit card surcharges. There is a US$2 per dive user fee in the marine reserves. There is a hyperbaric chamber at the Princess Margaret Hospital in Roseau.

ALDive, *Loubiere, T767-440 3483, www.al dive.com*. Diving, including courses, whale and dolphin watching, surfing, kayaks. Run by Billy and Samantha Lawrence.

Anchorage Dive Centre, *Anchorage Hotel, Castle Comfort, T767-448 2638, www.anchoragehotel.dm*, is based at the. This is another long-established operation with a good reputation, owned by Andrew Armour.

Cabrits Dive Centre, *operates from Picard Estate, Portsmouth, T767-445 3010, www.cabritsdive.com*. Diving and snorkelling in the less-visited north of the island.

Dive Dominica Ltd, *Castle Comfort Lodge, T767-448 2188, www.divedominica.com*. Offers full diving and accommodation packages, courses, single or multiple day dives, night dives and equipment rental, snorkelling and whale watching. Owned by the Perryman family, this is one of the most friendly and experienced operations, recommended for its professional service.

East Carib Dive Centre, *Salisbury, T767-499 6575, www.dominicadiving. com*. Owned and managed by Harald Zahn and Béatrice Contrera. Diving to the north and south, reached by 25-ft aluminium dive boat. Also offers hiking tours. Accommodation available with priority booking given to divers.

Nature Island Dive, *Soufrière, T767- 449 8181, www.natureislanddive.com*. Also snorkelling, kayaking and mountain biking, is run by a team of divers from around the world. Boat with platform for easy entry and exit. Ask about accommodation and dive packages; they have a bayside wooden cottage on stilts with porch for up to 4 divers, **Gallette**.

Fishing

Island Style, *T767-265 0518. www.island stylefishing.com*. Fishing charters from US$500 and whale-watching excursions US$55 per person.

Hiking

Hiking in the mountains is excellent, and hotels and tour companies arrange this type of excursion.

Lambert Charles, *T767-448 3365*. Strong on conservation and hiking, no office.

Kayaking and windsurfing

Ken's Hinterland Adventure Tours and Taxi Service (Khatts Ltd) (see below) offer river and sea kayaking tours.

Nature Island Dive (see Diving, above). Rents out sea kayaks, lifejackets and instruction in Soufrière Bay provided. Guided tours are available.

Wacky Rollers (see Adventure parks, above) offer guided river tubing and kayaking down the Layou River, Dominica's largest. Tours are geared to cruise ship visitors so check for availability beforehand.

Sailing

Gusty winds coming down from the hills make sailing difficult and unreliable; conditions are rarely suitable for beginners. The best harbour for yachts is Portsmouth (Prince Rupert Bay), but you should guard your possessions. Stealing from yachts is quite common. The jetty in Roseau is designed for small craft, such as yachts, clearing for port entry. Some hotels have moorings: **Fort Young** and **Anchorage** have moorings and a pier, and yachtsmen and women are invited to use the hotels' facilities.

Tour operators

Island tours can be arranged through many of the hotels.
Alfred Rolle, *Trafalgar Village, T767-448 7198*, or through **Papillote**. Personal tours; Alfred is extremely knowledgeable on the island and what lives on it and can tailor half-day and whole-day tours to suit clients.
Ken's Hinterland Adventure Tours and Taxi Service (Khatts Ltd), *Fort Young Hotel, Roseau, T767-448 4850, www.khattstours.com*. The most knowledgeable operators, lots of languages spoken, wide variety of tours and activities to suit all visitors.
Nature Island Destinations, *T767-449 6233, www.natureisland.com*. Arrange everything from accommodation to car hire, birdwatching, scuba diving and whale watching, for all budgets and tastes.
HHV Whitchurch & Co Ltd, *Old St, Roseau, T767-448 2181, see Facebook*. Handles local cruise ship passenger tours as well as foreign travel and represents American Express Travel Related Services, several airlines and L'Express des Iles.

Turtle watching

Dominica Sea Turtle Conservation Organization (DomSeTCO), see Facebook, monitors and protects nesting turtles and their hatchlings. They also have a hatchery for eggs in any nests they consider at risk. Call Simon (*T767-277 1608*), for information and if you want to watch turtle nesting on the beach. They work in conjunction with the **Rosalie Sea Turtle Initiative** (RoSTI) based at the Rosalie Bay Resort, see pages 100 and 105. Sea turtles start to arrive on Dominican beaches in Apr.

Whale watching

See Planning your trip, page 19. Whale-watching trips can be arranged with the **Anchorage Hotel** (Wed, Sat, Sun 1400-1800, US$57.50), **Dive Dominica** (Wed, Sun 1400), or **ALDive** (US$57.50). See also Diving, above.

Transport

Air

See Getting there, page 131, for details of airports and how to get to Dominica by air.

Boat

L'Express des Iles ferries operate from Roseau bayfront to **Fort-de-France** (1½ hrs), **Pointe-à-Pitre** (1¾ hrs) and **Castries** (3-3¾ hrs), see Getting there, page 132. Check timetables before planning a trip. The **L'Express des Iles** agency office (*T767-448 2181, www. express-des-iles.com*), is upstairs in the Whitchurch Centre.

Bus

Minibuses run from point to point. Those from Roseau to the northwest and northeast leave from between the east and west bridges near the modern market; to **Trafalgar** and Laudat from Valley Rd, near the Police HQ; for the south and **Petite Savane** from Old Market Place. They are difficult to get on early morning unless you can get on a 0630 bus out to the villages to pick up schoolchildren. Many buses pass the hotels south of Roseau.

Car

Driving is on the left. The steering wheel may be on either side.

If you are aged between 25 and 65, with 2 years' driving experience and a valid international or home driving licence, you may purchase a local driving permit, valid for 1 month, for US$12. The permit may be bought from the police at airports, rental agencies, or at the Traffic Dept, High St, Roseau or Bay St, Portsmouth (Mon to Fri).

Car hire   A car rental phone can be found at the airport and several of the companies will pick you up from there and help to arrange the licence. It is extremely difficult to hire a vehicle between Christmas and New Year, or at Carnival and Independence without prior reservation.

Courtesy Car Rental, *10 Winston Lane, Goodwill, Roseau, T767-4457677*, or at the airport *T767-4487763, www.dominicacar rentals.com*. Cars, jeeps, pick-ups and minivans, cheaper for longer, free pick up and drop off from either airport or ferry.

Island Car Rentals, *T767-255 6854, www. islandcar.dm*. Economy cars, jeeps, SUVs, minivans, pick-ups and trucks.

Valley, *T767-275 1310, www.valleyrent acar.com*. Offices at Melville Hall airport, Roseau and Portsmouth. 4WD jeeps, SUVs and minibuses.

Taxi

Taxis and minivans have HA or H on the licence plate. A sightseeing tour by taxi is economical if you have a group of 4 or more people and drivers can take you to waterfalls off the beaten track and sulphur springs as well as the more usual sights. Fares on set routes are fixed by the Government. **Nature Island Taxi Association** (*T767-448 1679*) and the **Dominica Taxi Association** (*T767-449 8533*) are the 2 main providers of taxis on the island. Ask at your hotel for a taxi and if you want one after 1800 you should arrange it in advance.

Background
St Lucia &
Dominica

St Lucia

Early history St Lucia was first settled by Arawaks in AD 200. By AD 800 their culture had been superseded by that of the Amerindian Caribs who called the island 'Iouanalao' and 'Hewanorra' meaning 'Island of the Iguanas'.

1502 It is believed that Christopher Columbus sailed past St Lucia but missed it completely.

1520 A Vatican globe marked the island as Santa Lucía, suggesting that it was claimed by Spain.

1605 The first European attempts to settle the island of Iouanalao, or Hewanorra, were repulsed by the Caribs. There is evidence of a Dutch expedition and also the arrival of 67 Englishmen en route to Guiana.

1638 The first recorded settlement was made by English from Bermuda and St Kitts but the colonists were killed by the Caribs about three years later.

1642 The King of France, claiming sovereignty over the island, ceded it to the French West India Company.

1650 The French West India Company sold the island to M Houel and M Du Parquet. There were several attempts by the Caribs to expel the French and several governors were murdered.

1660 The British began to renew their claim to the island and fighting for possession began in earnest. The settlers, mostly French, developed a plantation economy based on slave labour.

1762 British forces under Admiral George Rodney took St Lucia, only to lose it again in 1763.

1778 War erupted again. Admiral Rodney wrote that St Lucia was a far greater prize than neighbouring Martinique because of its excellent harbour, then called Carénage (now Castries).

1782 Admiral Rodney led the English fleet in an epic assault on the French navy, on its way to attack Jamaica. The Battle of Les Saintes took place around the French islands of Les Saintes and resulted in the death of some 14,000 French soldiers and sailors when Rodney broke the French formation, allowing his ships to encircle and fire broadsides into the helpless French vessels. The battle marked a turning point in the political balance of power and recognized British supremacy in the West Indies. However, in the subsequent Treaty of Versailles, St Lucia was returned to France and fighting continued intermittently.

ST LUCIA BACKGROUND
The first visitors

The first Amerindians to make the migration from the Orinoco and the northern coast of the Guianas arrived in St Lucia around AD 200, somewhat later than in the other islands of the Lesser Antilles. It is not known whether they bypassed St Lucia during earlier migrations or whether indeed they landed and their settlements are yet to be discovered by archaeologists. Remnants of the first settlers to arrive by canoe have been found at Grand Anse on the east coast and at Anse Noir in the south near Vieux Fort. They are now referred to as Island Arawaks, although Arawak refers to a language rather than a people. They stayed on St Lucia until around 1450, when they were replaced by the Caribs. No one yet knows what happened, whether they were killed, or driven out, but the pottery made by the Island Arawaks ceased to be made after that date and when the first European settlers arrived at the beginning of the 16th century, there were only Caribs in residence. Caribs survived here until the late 17th century but were then sent off to St Vincent and then to Central America. Nowadays only a small community survives on Dominica.

Even though some St Lucians have claimed that their island was discovered by Columbus on St Lucy's Day (13 December, the national holiday) in 1502, neither the date of discovery nor the discoverer are in fact known, for according to the evidence of Columbus' log, he appears to have missed the island and was not even in the area on St Lucy's Day. A Vatican globe of 1520 marks the island as Santa Lucía, suggesting that it was at least claimed by Spain. In 1605, 67 Englishmen en route to Guiana made an unsuccessful effort to settle, though a Dutch expedition may have discovered the island first. In 1638 the first recorded settlement was made by English from Bermuda and St Kitts, but the colonists were killed by the Caribs about three years later.

1796 During the French Revolution, Victor Hugues, used his base in St Lucia to support insurrections in nearby islands. The guillotine was erected in Castries and the island became known by the French as St Lucie La Fidèle. Britain invaded again and fought a protracted campaign against a guerrilla force of white and black republicans known as L'Armée Française dans les bois, until it was finally pacified by General John Moore.

1814 The Treaty of Paris awarded St Lucia to Britain and it became a British Crown Colony, having changed hands 14 times.

1834 Britain abolished slavery.

1838 The island was included in a Windward Islands Government, with a Governor resident first in Barbados and then in Grenada.

1885 St Lucia was chosen as one of Britain's two main coaling stations, selling Welsh coal to passing steam ships.

ST LUCIA BACKGROUND
Liberté, Fraternité, Egalité

After the French Revolution, activists entered St Lucia around the time that Haiti was undergoing its black Revolution and fomented civil unrest between slaves and planters. France abolished slavery in 1794, but a request for liberty by slaves on St Lucia was met by brutal repression by the local militia. The delay in implementing the emancipation was due to an English invasion about the time of the declaration. France and Britain were at war from 1793 and their colonies were part of the battlefield. A British expedition arrived in 1794 but were met by a revolt of white planters and free blacks. They formed the local Revolutionary Party and took to the hills, becoming known as L'Armée Française dans les bois, or brigands, with a stronghold in Soufrière. Guerrilla warfare brought the destruction of plantations all over the island and many bloody battles. In 1795 the British forces left their garrison in Castries to attack the revolutionaries at Soufrière. A French expedition from Guadeloupe came with reinforcements, a total of 600 troops and some cannon, to join the local fighting force of 250 St Lucians and 300 maroons, or escaped slaves, around the Fond Doux estate. The British marched overland from Vieux Fort and reached Fond Doux on 22 April, a week after leaving Castries, but they were ambushed in a heavy cross fire of cannon and musketry. After a day of fierce fighting the British retreated to Castries. They later suffered further defeats at Gros Islet and Vigie and on 19 June they fled, leaving the revolutionaries in control of the island. The slaves were freed, but a year later the British returned under the command of Generals Moore and Abercromby and in 1798 ended the brigand wars and brought back slavery.

1897 947 ships entered Castries harbour, 620 of them steam powered, and Castries was the fourteenth most important port in the world in terms of tonnage handled.

1935 The rise of oil brought the decline of coal. When coal workers went on strike, the Governor brought in a warship and marines patrolled the streets in a show of strength. No wage rises were granted.

1937 Sugar workers went on strike for higher wages. A small increase in wages was agreed.

1939 St Lucia's first trade union was formed, which grew into the St Lucia Labour Party (SLP), led by George FL Charles (1916-2004).

1951 Universal adult suffrage was introduced. The SLP won the elections and retained power until 1964. George Charles was the first Chief Minister. He pushed through several constitutional reforms, enhancing labour legislation for the benefit of workers and introducing the system of ministerial government. The sugar industry declined and bananas were promoted as suitable for smallholder production, eventually dominating the island's economy.

1958 St Lucia joined the short-lived West Indies Federation.

1964 The United Workers' Party (UWP) won the elections, led by Mr John Compton. He held power in 1964-1979 and subsequently won elections in 1982, 1987 and 1992.

1967 St Lucia gained full internal self-government, becoming a State in voluntary association with Great Britain. The first St Lucian Governor General was appointed, Sir Frederick Clarke (1912-1980), serving from 1967-1971.

1979 St Lucia gained full independence.

1996 Mr Compton retired as leader of the UWP and was replaced as Prime Minister and leader of the party by Dr Vaughan Lewis.

1997 The SLP triumphed in the elections, winning 16 of the 17 seats in the Assembly, and Dr Kenny Anthony became Prime Minister.

2001 The SLP was returned with a smaller majority, winning 14 seats. Its popularity had slipped in areas hit by the banana crisis and the world economic downturn with its knock-on effects on the tourism industry.

2004 When Sir George Charles, pioneer of the labour movement and the island's first Chief Minister, died on 26 June 2004, his body was put on view on the market steps at his own request.

2011 The general election was once again won by Dr Kenny Anthony of the SLP, who became prime minister for the second time on 30 November. The next elections are due in 2016.

Culture

There is a good deal of French cultural influence on St Lucia. Most of the islanders, who are predominantly of African descent (though a few people of Carib descent are still to be found in certain areas, noticeably around Choiseul). There is a French provincial style of architecture; most place names are French and about 70% of the population is Roman Catholic. The French Caribbean also has an influence on music, you can hear zouk and cadance played as much as calypso and reggae. The **Folk Research Centre** has recorded local music. *Musical Traditions of St Lucia* has 32 selections representing all the musical genres, with information on the background of the various styles. *Lucian Kaiso* is an annual publication giving pictures and information on each season of St Lucian calypso. In the pre-Christmas period, small drum groups play in rural bars. Traditionally, singers improvise a few lines about people and events in the community and the public joins in. The singing is exclusively in Kwéyòl, wicked and full of sexual allusions.

Language

The main language in St Lucia is English but 75% of the population also speak a patois, Lesser Antillean Créole French, called Kwéyòl. This is a language which evolved so that African slaves could communicate with their French masters and it has survived even though St Lucia has been British since 1814. It is similar to the Créole spoken in Haiti, Guadeloupe, Martinique and other former French colonies, but it is closest to the Kwéyòl of Dominica, another French island, which became British. It is said that Dominicans and St Lucians understand each other 98% of the time. Standard French, however, is understood by no more than 10% of St Lucians. Kwéyòl is a formal language, with grammar and syntax, but it has only recently been written down and many Kwéyòl speakers cannot in fact read it. It is spoken by St Lucians in all walks of life, including politicians, doctors, bankers, ministers and the Governor General, Dame Pearlette Louisy, who has done a great deal to promote it as a written language.

For people interested in learning a few phrases of Kwéyòl, there is a handwritten booklet by Mary Toynbee, *A Visitor's Guide to St Lucia Patois*, EC$20, and the *Kwéyòl Dictionary*, EC$10, published by the Ministry of Education, available in local bookshops. A visit to the market in Castries is one of the easiest ways to listen to Kwéyòl being spoken in the street or there are Kwéyòl programmes on the government information service, GIS.

Art

St Lucia has produced several painters of international renown. **Sir Dunstan St Omer** was born in St Lucia in 1927 into a Catholic family and is best known for his religious paintings. He created the altarpiece for the Jacmel church near Marigot Bay, where he painted his first black Christ, and reworked Castries Cathedral in 11 weeks in 1985 prior to the Pope's visit. St Omer and his four sons, Alwyn, Luigi, Giovanni and Julio, have also painted other countryside churches (Monchy and

Fond St Jacques) and a quarter of a mile of sea wall in Anse La Raye, while Giovanni and Julio installed the new windows in Castries cathedral.

Llewellyn Xavier was born in Choiseul in 1945 but moved to Barbados in 1961, where he discovered painting. Galleries in North America and Europe have exhibited his work and his paintings are in many permanent collections. Xavier returned to St Lucia in 1987, where he was shocked by the environmental damage. He has since campaigned vigorously for the environment through his art. *Environment Fragile* is a work created from recycled materials embedded with shards of pure gold and cannot be bought. It is given to those whose "voice can be heard above the din of global commerce".

Other outstanding artists include **Ron Savory**, whose rich rainforest scenes and dancing figures are impressive; **Sean Bonnett St Remy** paints wonderful local scenes, village scenes with nostalgic charm and accuracy; **Winston Branch** is splashy, modern abstract, and shows internationally from London to Brazil; **Chris Cox** paints St Lucian birds, such as the parrot and the nightjar. Other contemporary artists such as Arnold Toulon, Cedric George, Nancy Cole, Sophie Barnard, Alcina Nolley and Jonathon Gladding exhibit their works at the **Inner Gallery**.

Literature

One of the Caribbean's most renowned poets and playwrights in the English language, **Derek Walcott** (see box, page 35), was born in St Lucia in 1930. He has published many collections of poems, an autobiography in verse, *Another Life*, critical works, and plays such as *Dream on Monkey Mountain*. Walcott uses English poetic traditions, with a close understanding of the inner magic of the language (Robert Graves), to expose the historical and cultural facets of the Caribbean. His books are highly recommended, including his narrative poem *Omeros*, which contributed to his winning the 1992 Nobel Prize for Literature. Other St Lucian writers worth reading are the novelists **Garth St Omer** (*The Lights on the Hill*) and Earl Long (an MD in the USA), and the poets Jane King-Hippolyte, Kendal Hippolyte, John Robert Lee (*Artefacts*) and Jacintha Lee, who has a book of local legends. New authors to emerge in the 21st century include Anderson Reynolds, with his novel *Death By Fire*, and Michael Aubertin (head of the Department of Culture) with his period romance *Neg Maron*.

Land and environment

Geography

St Lucia is the second largest of the Windwards, lying between St Vincent and Martinique with an area of 238 square miles. The scenery is outstandingly beautiful, and in the neighbourhood of the Pitons, it has an element of grandeur. The highest peak is Morne Gimie, 3118 ft, but the most spectacular are Gros Piton, 2619 ft, and Petit Piton, 2461 ft, which are old volcanic forest-clad plugs rising sheer out of the sea near the town of Soufrière on the west coast. A few miles away is one of the world's most accessible volcanoes with *soufrières* (vents in the volcano which exude hydrogen sulphide, steam and other gases and deposit sulphur and other compounds in pools of boiling water). The mountains are intersected by numerous short rivers which in places debouch into broad, fertile and well-cultivated valleys.

Wildlife and plant life on St Lucia

For forest bird species, see box, page 55. The fauna and flora of St Lucia are very similar to that of Dominica, the Windward chain of islands having been colonized by plants and animals originally from South and Central America, with some endemic species. For instance, all the parrots of the islands are of the genus Amazona but most islands have a unique species such as the versicolor in St Lucia and the sisserou and imperialis in Dominica. Saint Lucia, like the other islands in the Windwards, would have at one time been covered by dense forest, but during colonization much of this was lost to agriculture. Today, what is left is protected to safeguard the island's water supply and its wildlife. Driving over the Barre de l'Isle or along the west coast road magnificent tree ferns, relics of prehistoric times, can be seen while on the roadside banks of wild ginger perfume the air. On the mountainsides the orange-red blossoms of the Imortelle light up the landscape. Many of the more exotic flowering plants, such as the hibiscus, the bougainvillea, the African tulip tree and the flamboyant were introduced during the establishment of the plantation system. Recent surveys have listed more than 1600 species of plants, including nine endemics.

Known locally as the **jacquot**, the St Lucia parrot is a very colourful bird with a green body, blue crown, turquoise cheeks and scarlet breast. They were seriously endangered a few years ago because of hunting, both for food and the pet trade, and competition from other birds for their habitat. Many of their nesting sites were destroyed by hurricanes and their population faced extinction in the 1970s. However, a concerted effort to save them through protection, education and breeding has raised the numbers to over 800 in the wild now. They are best seen in the wild in the mountains around Quillesse, Edmund Forest and Millet, but for a close up view there are several in cages at Union Zoo (page 39).

The **iguana** is the largest of the lizards found on St Lucia, growing up to 6 ft long including the tail. It is mostly green, with brown or black stripes, nose horns and a crest of long spines along the neck. Females lay up to 17 eggs in the ground, which take around 14 weeks to hatch. Iguanas are vegetarians, eating leaves, shoots and fruit. They live in trees but can also be seen on the ground. There are several iguanas at Union Zoo, but in the wild they are found on the northeast coast around Louvet and Grand Anse. Numbers are decreasing because of predation by mongooses and feral cats. Other reptile species include the St Lucia tree lizard, pygmy gecko and Maria Islands ground lizard, all endemic.

There are four species of **snake** on the island. The only one that is dangerous is the fer-de-lance, which is restricted to dry scrub woodland on the east coast near Grand Anse and Louvet and also near Anse La Raye and Canaries in the west. Attacks are rare. The bite is not fatal but requires hospitalization. Avoid walking through the bush, especially at night, and wear shoes or boots and long trousers.

The largest snake on the island is the **boa**, also called tètchyen. It grows up to 14 ft long and lives on small prey that it suffocates in its coils. In the wild they live in the drier areas of the island and can often be seen asleep in trees. There are a couple kept at Union Zoo and you sometimes see men displaying them at the roadside as a tourist attraction. The other two species are the Maria Island grass snake and the tiny, blindworm snake.

The largest group of mammals is made up of six or more species of **bat**. These include fruit eating, insect eating and even fishing bats. The cave on the northern side of the bay approaching Soufrière is home to thousands. They emerge at dusk.

A member of the rodent family, the **agouti** is a mammal indigenous to St Lucia. It has coarse brown hair and sits erect on long thin legs. The agouti is nocturnal, living in open country on the edge of forests and feeding on leaves, roots, fruit and nuts. It reproduces twice a year, having two or three babies in each litter, which are born fully active. Like all St Lucia's wildlife (except the fer-de-lance, mongoose, rats and mice), agoutis were declared a protected species in 1980 after they became scarce, but there are several in Union Zoo which have been born in captivity. Although the agouti is rarely seen, the manicou is present throughout the island, but is frequently seen on the road, a victim of the night time traffic. The mongoose, first introduced into Jamaica in 1872 to control the rats in the canefields, is also present.

Dominica

Early history As on the other islands in the Windward chain, there were waves of migration from the Orinoco Delta area of South America up through the island arc to the Greater Antilles. The Caribs, who supplanted the Arawaks on Dominica, called the island Waitikubuli ('tall is her body').

1493 Columbus sighted Dominica on 3 November 1493, a Sunday (hence the current name), but the Spanish took no interest in the island.

1660 The island was fought over by the French, British and Caribs. In 1660, the two European powers agreed to leave Dominica to the Caribs, but the arrangement lasted very few years.

1686 The island was declared neutral, again, with little success. As France and England renewed hostilities, the Caribs were divided between the opposed forces and suffered the heaviest losses in consequence.

1763 Dominica was ceded to Britain.

1805 Possession was finally settled. Nevertheless, its position between the French colonies of Guadeloupe and Martinique, and the strong French presence over the years, ensured that despite English institutions and language the French influence was never eliminated. During the 19th century, Dominica was largely neglected and underdevelopment provoked social unrest.

1899 Henry Hesketh Bell (colonial administrator 1899-1905), made great improvements to infrastructure and the economy.

1930s The British government's Moyne Commission discovered a return to a high level of poverty on the island. Assistance to the island was increased with some emphasis put on road building to open up the interior. This, together with agricultural expansion, house building and use of the abundant hydro resources for power, contributed to development in the 1950s and 1960s.

1939 Dominica was transferred from the Leeward to the Windward Islands Federation.

1960 Dominica gained separate status and a new constitution. The Dominica Labour Party dominated island politics after 1961, ushering in all the constitutional changes.

1967 Dominica gained full internal autonomy.

ON THE ROAD

Dame Eugenia Charles

Dame Eugenia Charles (1919-2005) was a formidable woman, leading her party, the Dominican Freedom Party (DFP) from 1968 until her retirement in 1995 aged 76. The Commonwealth of Dominica became an independent republic within the Commonwealth in 1978 and Dame Eugenia won consecutive general elections in 1980, just after Hurricane David devastated the island in 1979, 1985 and 1990, becoming the Caribbean's first woman prime minister. It was she who invited the USA to invade Grenada after the murder of Prime Minister Maurice Bishop in 1983, subsequently appearing on television with President Reagan and earning the sobriquet of the Caribbean's 'Iron Lady', although at home in Dominica she was more affectionately known as 'Mamo' and never encouraged the cult of personality.

1978 The Commonwealth of Dominica became an independent republic within the Commonwealth.

1980 Following Independence, internal divisions and public dissatisfaction with the administration led to its defeat by the Dominica Freedom Party in the 1980 elections. The DFP Prime Minister, Miss (now Dame) Eugenia Charles, adopted a pro-business, pro-United States line to lessen the island's dependence on limited crops and markets.

1985 Charles was re-elected in 1985 and again in 1990, having survived an earlier attempted invasion by supporters of former DLP premier, Patrick John.

1995 Charles retired at the age of 76, having led her party since 1968. The general election was won by the United Workers Party (UWP) and Mr Edison James was sworn in as Prime Minister.

2000 The general elections in 2000 gave the Dominica Labour Party (DLP) 42.9%, the UWP 43.4% and the DFP 13.6% of the vote. The DLP and DFP formed a coalition and on 3 February Mr Rosie Douglas was sworn in as Prime Minister. However, the country was stunned by his death, aged 58, in 2000. He was replaced by his deputy, Pierre Charles.

2004-present Pierre Charles died suddenly in January 2004. Charles was replaced by Roosevelt Skerrit, who became the world's youngest prime minister at age 31 and has remained prime minister ever since. The next elections are due in 2018.

Culture

The island's mountainous terrain discourages the creation of large estates and so there are many small farmers. In Dominica, over 2000 descendants of the original inhabitants of the Caribbean, the once warlike Caribs, live in the Carib Territory, a 3700-acre 'reservation' established in 1903 in the northeast. The total population is otherwise almost entirely of African descent. Catholicism predominates, though there are some Methodist and Protestant denominations and an increasing number of fundamentalist sects, imported from the USA.

Language
Like St Lucia, Dominica was once a French possession and although English is the official tongue, most of the inhabitants also speak Kwéyòl (French-based patois). Dominicans are proud of their local language, which is increasingly being used in print. A dictionary was published in 1991 and is updated by the Konmité pou Etid Kwéyòl (Committee for Créole Studies). There are no surviving speakers of the Carib language on the island. In the Marigot/Wesley area a type of English called kokoy is used; the original settlers of the area, freed slaves, came from Antigua and are mostly Methodists.

Literature
The best known of Dominica's writers are the novelists **Jean Rhys** and **Phyllis Shand Allfrey**. Rhys (1894-1979), who spent much of her life in Europe and wrote mainly about that continent; only flashback scenes in *Voyage in the Dark* (1934), her superb last novel, *Wide Sargasso Sea* (1966, which was made into a film in 1991), her uncompleted autobiography, *Smile Please*, and resonances in some of her short stories draw on her West Indian experiences. Allfrey published only one novel, *The Orchid House* (1953); *In the Cabinet* was left unfinished at her death in 1986. Allfrey was one of the founder members of the Dominica Labour Party, became a cabinet minister in the short-lived West Indian Federation, and was later editor of the *Dominica Herald* and *Dominica Star* newspapers. *The Orchid House* was filmed by Channel 4 (UK) in 1990 for international transmission as a four-part series. For a history of the island, see *The Dominica Story*, by Lennox Honychurch.

Land and environment

Geography
Dominica is one of the largest and most mountainous of the anglophone Windward Islands. It is 29 miles long and 16 miles wide, with an area of 290 sq miles. The highest peak, Morne Diablotin, rises to 4747 ft and is often shrouded in mist. It is known as the Nature Island of the Caribbean with parks and reserves protecting vast areas of forest that cover most of the interior. The rainy season is from July to November though showers occur all through the year. Note that the mountains are much wetter and cooler than the coast. In addition, the frequent

rainfall and many rivers have led to some very dramatic seascapes with beautiful hard and soft coral.

Dominica's protected areas

The Forestry, Wildlife and National Parks Division (FWP) is responsible for the management of forest reserves and national parks as well as the conservation and protection of Dominica's wild flora and fauna. While about 60% of the island is forested, most of this is privately owned. About 20% of the land is under some sort of legal protected status, comprising the Northern Forest Reserve and the Central Forest Reserve, together covering 5688 ha, and the three national parks of Morne Trois Pitons (a UNESCO World Heritage Site), Morne Diablotin and Cabrits, amounting to 10,746 ha. The Cabrits National Park also includes a 426-ha marine reserve, while the main marine protected area is the Soufrière-Scotts Head Marine Reserve surrounding the Scotts Head Peninsula.

At the highest levels on the island is elfin woodland, characterized by dense vegetation and low-growing plants. Elfin woodland and high montane thicket give way to rainforest at altitudes between 330 m and 800 m. The Morne Trois Pitons Reserve has the richest biodiversity in the Lesser Antilles. It contains five volcanoes, on the slopes of which there are 50 fumaroles and hot springs, freshwater lakes and a 'boiling lake'.

The twin hills of the Cabrits Peninsula in the northwest are covered by dry forest. It is separated from the island by marshland which is a nesting place for herons and doves and hosts a variety of migrant bird species. A walk through the woods and around the buildings of Fort Shirley will reveal much flora and wildlife. The scuttling hermit (or soldier) and black crabs, ground lizard (abòlò) and tree lizard are most visible.

Wildlife and plant life on Dominica

In addition to the huge variety of trees, many of which flower in March and April, there are orchids and wild gardens in the valleys. **Bwa Kwaib** or Carib wood (*Sabinea carinalis*) is the national flower; found mostly growing along parts of the west coast.

Indigenous birds to the island are the **imperial parrot**, or sisserou (*Amazona imperialis*), which is critically endangered, and its marginally less threatened relative, the red-necked parrot, or **Jacquot** (*Amazona arausiaca*). The sisserou is the national bird. They can be seen in the Syndicate area in the northwest, which is now a protected reserve (accessible by 4WD only). There is a nature trail but signs are difficult to spot. The parrots are most evident during their courting season, in April and early May. To get the best from a parrot-watching trip, it is worth taking a guide. While there are other rare species, such as the forest thrush and the blue-headed hummingbird, there are a great many others which are easily spotted (the purple-throated carib and Antillean-crested hummingbirds, for instance), or heard (the *siffleur montagne*). Waterfowl can be seen on the lakes, waders on the coastal wetlands (many are migrants).

There are fewer species of **mammal** (agouti, manicou-opossum, wild pig and bats in caves, most particularly at Thiband on the northeast coast), but there is a wealth of insect life (for example, over 55 species of butterfly) and **reptiles**. There is the rare iguana, the *crapaud* (a large frog known as 'mountain chicken') and five snakes, none poisonous (includes the boa constrictor, or *tête-chien*). Certain parts of the coast are used as nesting grounds by sea turtles (hawksbill, leatherback and green).

Practicalities
St Lucia &
Dominica

Getting there

Air

St Lucia

The island is well served by scheduled and charter flights from Europe and North America and you can often pick up quite cheap deals on package holidays. Connections with other islands are good and it is easy to arrange a multi-centre trip. Some flights come via Antigua, Barbados or the French Antilles.

St Lucia has two airports: **George F Charles Airport** (SLU – formely Vigie) ⓘ *T758-452 1156*, mainly for short-hop inter-island flights only (2 miles from Castries), and **Hewanorra International Airport** (UVF) ⓘ *T758-4546355*, in the Vieux Fort district (40 miles from Castries). There is an air shuttle between the two by helicopter, 10 minutes, US$165 per person, or 15 minutes, US$180 for a more scenic route around the Pitons and Soufrière, www.stluciahelicopters.com. A taxi will cost you US$70 for up to three passengers to Castries/Vigie airport, US$75 to Rodney Bay, US$85 to Cap Estate, US$70 to Soufrière. It will take you 1½ to two hours by car to reach Rodney Bay and the resorts north of Castries, either by the scenic new west coast road or the road up the wilder Atlantic side. You can sometimes negotiate a ride with one of the transfer buses from hotels for less, enquire at **St Lucia Reps** ⓘ *T758-456 9100, www.stluciareps.com*. They also offer other transfer services, including limousines, private minibuses, shared minibuses and private cars, with advance booking. If you are travelling light you can walk to the main road and catch the minibus or route taxi to Castries, or if you are staying in Vieux Fort you can walk there, but be careful of the fast traffic.

Dominica

There are no direct flights from Europe or North America to Dominica. Connections must be made in Puerto Rico, St Maarten, Antigua, Barbados or the French Antilles. Connecting air services are provided by LIAT, **Seabourne Airlines**, in a code-share agreement with American Eagle, Winair and **Air Sunshine**. If you are coming from Europe it is worth investigating flights from France to Martinique and then catching the ferry (see below) from Fort-de-France, which is cheaper than flying.

Dominica also has two airports, **Melville Hall** (DOM) in the northeast, which handles most planes, and **Canefield** (DCF) near Roseau, which takes only very small aircraft such as courier services and charter air taxi services such as Hummingbird Air. Melville Hall is 36 miles from Roseau and takes about one to 1½ hours to drive, or more if there are roadworks or traffic congestion. From Melville Hall to Roseau or Portsmouth is EC$65/US$26. If you don't find someone to share it with it will be assumed you want the vehicle to yourself, and you pay for the whole car.

Sea

While St Lucia, Dominica and Martinique are on the itineraries of very many cruise lines and lots of private or chartered yachts also call during a tour of the Lesser Antilles, the main transport link between the three islands is by international ferry.

Express des Iles

Express des Iles ⓘ *www.express-des-iles.com*, has daily services connecting Guadeloupe, Les Saintes, Marie Galante, Dominica, Martinique and St Lucia. Immigration and customs formalities and departure taxes have to be complied with at each country and check-in is 1½ hours before departure.

In **St Lucia**, the ferry terminal is on La Toc Road, Castries. Departure tax is EC$33. The ticket agent, **Cox & Company Ltd** ⓘ *Mon-Fri 0800-1615, T758-456 5022-4, credit cards accepted*, has an office there.

In **Dominica**, the ferry terminal is on the bayfront, Roseau, and tickets can be purchased from the office in the **Whitchurch Centre** ⓘ *T767-448 2181*. Departure tax EC$59, paid in cash. In Fort-de-France, Martinique, the ferry operates from the Terminal Interlles, and the ticket agency is **Brudey Frères** ⓘ *T596-(0)596-700850*. All ferry terminals are in walking distance of the town centre and within easy reach of bus routes, although taxis are available.

Ferries leave **Castries** Monday, Thursday and Sunday for Roseau with a stop in Fort-de-France. On other days it is not possible to get there in one day as the ferry for Roseau leaves Fort-de-France before the ferry comes in from Castries, so you have to have an overnight stop in Martinique.

From **Roseau** to Castries the only day you can do the journey in one day is Friday (and some Saturdays). Check the schedule as it is subject to change. If you are planning to fly home from St Lucia after a trip to Dominica do not plan to catch the ferry on the same day as your flight, always leave yourself a day in hand in case of delays and cancellations. International fares in 2015 were €79 one way, €119 return, with discounts for children, pensioners and families.

Getting around

Road

Roads are generally in good condition after considerable investment in improvements in the last few years. However, in mountainous areas they remain susceptible to landslides after storms, and in urban areas they can be heavily congested. Journey times are often quoted in hours rather than miles, as driving on twisty, hilly roads is time-consuming.

St Lucia has a very busy main road heading north out of Castries to the resort area, while the road south down the scenic West Coast Road is less congested, but the terrain requires slow driving. The East Coast Road has been repaired following hurricane damage but is the route taken by goods vehicles between Vieux Fort and Castries. These two roads, together with the Transinsular Road over the Barre de l'Isle mountains in the middle of the island, make a lovely circular route.

Dominica's roads have recently benefitted from Chinese finance and manpower. The road north from Roseau to the second city of Portsmouth is an attractive drive along the coast. From here you can cross over to the east coast for a spectacular view of the Atlantic side of the island, either turning inland on the Transinsular Road to Pont Cassé, Canefield and Roseau, or going further south to either Castle Bruce or Rosalie before taking alternative roads to the Pont Cassé roundabout. Roads in the southern third of the island are not all so well maintained.

Bus

Getting around St Lucia by bus is easy and the cheapest way of getting around. Hotels and tour operators will encourage you to take a taxi, but this is quite unnecessary during the day unless you want to get to somewhere off the beaten track. The service has been described as tiresome by some, but as reliable by others. St Lucia's minibuses have the letter M on their licence plates, are usually privately owned and have no fixed timetable. The north is better served than the south and buses around Castries and Gros Islet run until 2200, or later for the Friday night jump-up at Gros Islet. There are more buses in the morning than later on in the day, so don't leave it too late to make your return trip. Bus stands in Castries are on Darling Road at the end of Jn Baptiste Street for the north, on the south side of the market for Anse-la-Raye and the southwest, and from Hospital Road on the south side of the river for Vieux Fort and Dennery. Route 1 is Castries to Gros Islet, Route 2 Castries to Vieux Fort, Route 3 Castries to Soufrière, Route 4 Vieux Fort environs, Route 5 Castries central zone. Each route then has sub-routes. Short journeys are only EC$1.50, rising to EC$8 Castries to Soufrière. Ask the driver to tell you when your stop comes up.

In Dominica, minibuses run from point to point, 0600-1900, although there are only a few on Sundays. They are identified from other minibuses by the letter H on the licence plate. Those from Roseau to the northwest and northeast leave from between the east and west bridges near the modern market; to Trafalgar and Laudat from Valley Road near the Police HQ; for the south and Petitie Savane from Old Market Place. They are difficult to get on early morning unless you can get on a 0630 bus out to the villages to pick up schoolchildren. Many buses pass the hotels south of Roseau. Fares are fixed by the Government, starting at EC$2 for a short journey, to EC$9 to Portsmouth and EC$11 to Marigot.

Car

Drive on the left although the steering wheel may be on either side. Take care at roundabouts if you are not used to them and give way to traffic coming from your right. The use of seat belts is compulsory.

The speed limit on St Lucia is 30 mph on highways, 15 mph in towns, although you will be lucky to find anyone keeping to those limits. It is illegal to drive on beaches. Castries roads are very congested and there are many one-way streets. There are several car hire companies on the island, some of which are open to negotiation, but it is cheaper and more reliable to hire in advance. Car hire is about US$50-100 per day, depending on the size of the vehicle, with discounts for weekly rates. The minimum age for car rental is 25. A temporary local driving permit costs US$22. If arriving at George F L Charles (formerly Vigie) Airport, get your international licence endorsed at the immigration desk (closed 1300-1500) after going through customs. Car hire companies can usually arrange a licence. Most have offices at the hotels, airports and in Castries. Check for charges for pick-up and delivery.

In Dominica, speed limits in urban areas are posted in kilometres per hour, but there are no official limits in the countryside. You should take care as the roads are hilly, drops can be precipitous, there are many blind corners and roads can be slippery after rain. Avoid driving after dark as street lighting is minimal and the terrain is hazardous for the uninitiated. A 4WD vehicle is recommended and most hire companies have more of them than saloon cars. If you are aged between 25 and 65, with two year's driving experience, you may purchase a local driving permit, valid for one month, for US$12, for which a valid international or home driving licence is required. The permit may be bought from the police at airports, rental agencies, or at the Traffic Department, High Street, Roseau or Bay Street, Portsmouth (Monday to Friday). Car hire rates are about US$60 per day for a car and US$70 for a jeep; unlimited mileage for hiring for three days or more. A car rental phone can be found at the airport and several of the companies will pick you up from there and help to arrange the licence. It is extremely difficult to hire a vehicle between Christmas and New Year, or at Carnival and Independence without prior reservation. See also Dominica Transport, page 114.

Cycling

Cycling on the islands is a tough work-out, with steep hills and tight curves. It is also potentially dangerous, with pot holes to avoid, traffic coming round a bend on the wrong side of the road and no space to get off the road. However, the views are tremendous and there is good cycling both on- and off-road.

The best way to get around St Lucia by bike is anti-clockwise, ensuring long but gradual uphills and steep, fast downhills. Off-road, there are purpose-built trails for different levels of ability at Anse Mamin Plantation, part of the **Anse Chastenet Resort** ⓘ *www.bikestlucia.com*.

Cycling is growing in popularity on Dominica and the island's roads, although twisty, are good. Traffic is generally light with the exception of the stretch from Roseau to Layou. Between Canefield and Pont Cassé it is very steep, twisty and challenging. So do not cycle after dark, be aware of traffic overtaking you far too close and look out for potholes. Roads can be very slippery after rain. Take food and plenty of water with you, a puncture repair kit and a mobile phone. Cyclists visiting Dominica should contact Joel Challenger, Secretary of the **Dominica Cycling Association** ⓘ *T767-615 5675, see Facebook*.

Taxi

Registered taxis in St Lucia have red number plates with the TX prefix. Minibuses have the T prefix. Fares are set by the government, but always verify the rate before embarking on a journey and make sure you are being quoted in EC$, not US$. Fare from Castries to Gros Islet, US$25; Rodney Bay to Gros Islet or Pigeon Island National Park, US$10; taxi for a day's sightseeing, US$200-250 (see above for fares from the airport). If in doubt about the amount charged, check with the tourist office or hotel reception. You can see a copy of the fixed fares at the airport. At rush hour it is almost impossible to get a taxi so allow plenty of time, the traffic jams are amazing for such a small place. Taxi drivers are generally very knowledgeable about the island and make good tour guides.

In Dominica, taxis and minivans have HA, HB or H on the licence plate. Fares on set routes are fixed by the Government. Ask at your hotel for a taxi and if you want one after 1800 you should arrange it in advance. The fare from Roseau to Canefield is EC$25/US$10.

Walking

Hiking is particularly rewarding on both St Lucia and Dominica as the views are stunning and there are lots of birds and plants to see. There are many trails for hiking of varying degrees of difficulty through the mountains and the rainforest. There are guides and organized hiking tours if you don't want to go it alone. If you are walking along the road, remember to walk on the right so that you can see approaching vehicles. Avoid walking on the road at night as there is often nowhere to get off and oncoming cars travel very fast.

Essentials A-Z

Accident and emergency

T911 in St Lucia, T911 or 999 in Dominica.

Electricity

220 volts, 50 cycles. A few hotels are 110 v, 60 cycles. Most sockets take 3-pin square plugs (UK standard), but some take 2-pin round plugs or flat US plugs. Adaptors generally available in hotels.

Embassies and consulates

For a full list of embassies and consulates in St Lucia and Dominica and St Lucian and Dominican offices abroad, see http://embassy.goabroad.com.

Health

Travel in St Lucia and Dominica poses no health risk to the average visitor provided sensible precautions are taken. It is important to see your GP or travel clinic at least 6 weeks before departure for general advice on any travel risks and necessary vaccinations. Try phoning a specialist travel clinic if your own doctor is unfamiliar with health conditions in the Windward Islands. Check with your national health service or health insurance on coverage in the islands and take a copy of your insurance policy with you. Also get a dental check, know your own blood group and if you suffer a long-term condition such as diabetes or epilepsy, obtain a Medic Alert bracelet/necklace (www.medicalert. co.uk). If you wear glasses, take a copy of your prescription.

Vaccinations

It is important to confirm your primary courses and boosters are up to date. It is also advisable to vaccinate against **tetanus**, **typhoid** and **hepatitis A**. Vaccines sometimes advised are **hepatitis B**, **rabies** and **diphtheria**. **Yellow fever** vaccination is not required unless you are coming directly from an infected country in Africa or South America. Although **cholera** vaccination is largely ineffective, immigration officers may ask for proof of such vaccination if coming from a country where an epidemic has occurred. Check www.who.int for updates. **Malaria** is not a danger in St Lucia or Dominica.

Health risks

The most common affliction of travellers to any country is probably diarrhoea and the same is true of St Lucia and Dominica. Tap water is good in most areas, but bottled water is widely available and recommended. Swimming in sea or river water that has been contaminated by sewage can be a cause of diarrhoea; ask locally if it is safe. Diarrhoea may also be caused by viruses, bacteria (such as E-coli), protozoal (such as giardia), salmonella and cholera. It may be accompanied by vomiting or by severe abdominal pain. Any kind of diarrhoea responds well to the replacement of water and salts. Sachets of rehydration salts can be bought in most chemists and can be dissolved in boiled water. If the symptoms persist, consult a doctor.

The major risks posed in the region are those caused by insect disease carriers such as mosquitoes and sandflies. The key parasitic and viral diseases are dengue fever and chikungunya (also known as chik V). **Dengue fever** and **chikungunya** are particularly hard to protect against as the mosquitoes can bite throughout the day as well as night (unlike those that carry malaria). Chikungunya virus is relatively new in the Caribbean but there has been an outbreak in both St Lucia and Dominica. There is no malaria. There are lots of mosquitoes at certain times of the year, so take insect repellent and avoid being bitten as much as possible. Sleep off the ground and use a mosquito net and some kind of insecticide. Remember that DEET (Di-ethyltoluamide) is the gold standard. Apply the repellent every 4-6 hrs but more often if you are sweating heavily. If a non-DEET product is used, check who tested it. Validated products (tested at the London School of Hygiene and Tropical Medicine) include Mosiguard, Non-DEET Jungle formula and non-DEET Autan. If you want to use citronella remember that it must be applied very frequently (ie hourly) to be effective.

The climate is hot; the islands are tropical and protection against the sun will be needed. Do not be deceived by cooling sea breezes. To reduce the risk of sunburn and skin cancer, make sure you pack high-factor sun cream, light-coloured loose clothing and a hat.

If you get sick

There are hospitals, medical centres and clinics around St Lucia, while the larger hotels have doctors on call. Dominica has several public hospitals and private clinics and a hyperbaric chamber. Make sure you have adequate insurance (see below). Remember you cannot dial any toll-free numbers abroad so make sure you have a contact number.

St Lucia

In an emergency call T911 or go to the **Gros Islet PolyClinic**, T758-450 9661, Mon-Fri 0800-1630. **Victoria Hospital**, Castries, T758-452 2421/453 7059. **St Jude's**, Vieux Fort, T758-454 6041. **Soufrière Casualty**, T758-459 7258. **Dennery**, T758-453 3310. **Tapion**, T758-459 2000, 24-hr emergency service, pay first, treatment later, expensive, pharmacy, X-ray, CAT scan, laboratory services, specialist doctors. **Rodney Bay Medical Centre**, T758-452 8621, is a collection of private doctors and dentists. Larger hotels have resident doctors or doctors 'on call', visits cost about EC$70-100. If given a prescription, ask at the pharmacy whether the medication is available 'over the counter', as this may be cheaper.

Dominica

There are 3 public hospitals on the island: the **Marigot Hospital**, T767-445 7091, the **Portsmouth Hospital**, T767-445 5237, and the **Princess Margaret Hospital**, T767-448 2231. Casualty and intensive care units are available at the Portsmouth Hospital and the Princess Margaret Hospital (PMH). The PMH also has a hyperbaric chamber. Several specialists and general practitioners operate private clinics. **Hillborough St Clinic** is quite large with pharmacy attached. Note that you have to pay in advance for everything.

Useful websites

www.bgtha.org British Global and Travel Health Association.

www.cdc.gov Centers for Disease Control and Prevention; US government site that gives excellent advice on travel health and details of disease outbreaks.
www.fco.gov.uk British Foreign and Commonwealth Office travel site has useful information on each country, people, climate and a list of UK embassies/consulates.
www.fitfortravel.scot.nhs.uk A-Z of vaccine/health advice for each country.

Insurance

All travellers should hold comprehensive travel insurance including medical insurance. Insurance should be valid for the full duration of your stay and should cover medical evacuation. You should check any exclusions, and that your policy covers you all for the activities you want to undertake, such as scuba diving or canyoning.

Language

English is the official language but Kwéyòl, a French-based patois, is spoken widely on both St Lucia and Dominica. It is very similar to the Créole of Martinique and Haiti. See also pages 121 and 127.

Money

The currency on both islands is the East Caribbean dollar, EC$, fixed at EC$2.67 = US$1.

Exchange
Banks will exchange major currencies, such as the US$, Can$, € and £. Some traders will accept US$, but you will get a better rate if you change your money at a bank. You will receive your change in EC$.

Plastic/Banks (ATMs)
Credit cards are accepted in the larger hotels, restaurants and shops, but cafés, rum shops and smaller operators only take cash. Banks nearly all have ATMs and accept all major international cards.

Cost of living/travelling
The islands are expensive, reflecting the need to import most daily essential items and the lack of any economies of scale. High season is Dec-Apr, when hotel prices are at their highest. Good deals can be found in hurricane season, particularly Sep-Nov. Cheap and cheerful lodging can be found on St Lucia for US$40-50 a night, but it will be inland, not on the beach. Generally, a room in a decent hotel or guesthouse will cost in the region of US$100 a night, or more for the luxury places. On Dominica there is camping or dorm rooms at 3 Rivers and at some guesthouses in the off season for less than US$30, but generally you should expect to pay a lot more in a hotel. Some of the cheaper accommodation can only be reached with a rental car, unless you are in the city, which can be noisy, hot and uncomfortable. Renting a house or apartment is an option for a group so you can share the cost. Eating in local cafeterias, drinking in rum shops and travelling on buses can save you money.

Opening hours

St Lucia
Banks Mon-Thu 0800-1400, Fri 0800-1700, in Rodney Bay banks open on Sat until 1200.
Government offices Mon-Fri 0830-1230, 1330-1600.
Shops Mon-Fri 0800-1700, although

a few shut for lunch, Sat 0800-1230, supermarkets stay open later.

Dominica

Banks Mon-Thu 0800-1400, Fri 0800-1700.
Government offices Mon-Fri 0800-1300, 1400-1600
Shops Mon-Fri 0800-1300, 1400-1600, Sat 0800-1300. Many supermarkets in Roseau now stay open at lunch and some until 2000.

Public holidays

St Lucia

1 and 2 Jan **New Year**
22 Feb **Independence Day**
Easter **Good Friday**, **Easter Monday**
1 May **Labour Day**
May/June **Whit Monday; Corpus Christi**
July **Carnival**
1 Aug **Emancipation Day**
1st Mon in Oct **Thanksgiving Day**
13 Dec **National Day**
25 and 26 Dec **Christmas Day** and **Boxing Day.**

Dominica

1 and 2 Jan **New Year**. A merchant's holiday takes place on 2 Jan, when all shops and restaurants and most government offices are closed, although banks and hotels stay open
Feb/Mar **Carnival**
Easter **Good Friday** and **Easter Monday**
May/June **first monday; Whit Monday**
Aug **1st Monday**
3-4 Nov **Independence**
25 and 26 Dec **Christmas Day** and **Boxing Day**

Safety

The islands are relatively safe but you still need to exercise caution, especially against petty theft, which should always be reported to the police. Do not leave your possessions unattended on the beach; leave valuables in the hotel safe and if renting a car, keep everything out of sight and locked in the boot. Don't offer lifts to strangers. Street lighting is patchy so avoid dark streets at night. Do not go to out of the way or deserted beaches at night and do not sleep on the beach.

Tax

Departure tax on St Lucia of EC$68/US$26 and an airport development charge of US$35 are included in the price of your air ticket, although if you are leaving on the ferry there is a departure tax of EC$33. Departure tax on Dominica is EC$59/US$22 for anyone aged 12 and over.

Telephone

The international code for St Lucia is 758 and for Dominica 767.

Time

Atlantic Standard Time: GMT -4 hrs, EST + 1 hr.

Tipping

Tipping is welcomed by all hospitality staff. At restaurants a service charge of 10-15% is often included, but you can leave whatever you wish. Hotel porters should be tipped according to how many bags they carry. You may find you get better service if the person who cleans your room is left a small, daily tip. Taxis should also be tipped.

Tourist information

Local tourist offices can be found at the start of the listings sections on pages 58 (St Lucia) and 101 (Dominica).
The **St Lucia Tourist Board** has information bureaux at the airports (open when flights arrive) and the cruise ship ports (open when a cruise ship is in) for advice and brochures. For offices in the UK, USA and Canada, see http://stlucianow.co.uk/contact.
Discover Dominica Authority has offices and representation in the USA, Canada, UK, Europe and Scandinavia, see www.dominica.dm/index.php/contact-us.

Vaccinations

No vaccination certificates are required except for yellow fever if you are coming from an infected area.

Visas and immigration

All foreign nationals arriving in St Lucia and Dominica must have a valid passport. Visitors from the UK, the USA, Canada, most European countries, the Commonwealth and some other nations do not need visas. For a full list, see http://archive.stlucia.gov.lc/faq/index.htm and http://www.dominica.gov.dm/services/what-are-the-entry-requirements-for-the-commonwealth-of-dominica/do-i-need-a-visa-to-enter-into-dominica.

Weights and measures

Metric and imperial.

Index

Entries in bold refer to maps

Credits

Footprint credits
Editor: Nicola Gibbs
Production and layout: Patrick Dawson
Maps: Kevin Feeney
Colour section: Angus Dawson

Publisher: Patrick Dawson
Managing Editor: Felicity Laughton
Administration: Elizabeth Taylor
Advertising sales and marketing:
John Sadler, Kirsty Holmes
Business Development: Debbie Wylde

Photography credits
Front cover:
Darryl Brooks/Shutterstock.com
Back cover: Top: Richard Goldberg/
Shutterstock.com. Bottom: Kendra
Nielsen/Shutterstock.com.

Colour section
Inside front cover: Stephanie Rousseau/
Shutterstock.com; BlueGreen Pictures/
SuperStock.com; T photography/
Shutterstock.com. **Page 1**: Wolfgang
Kaehler/SuperStock.com. **Page 2**:
Mikadun/Shutterstock.com. **Page
4**: Styve Reineck/Shutterstock.com;
National Geographic/SuperStock.com;
Biosphoto/SuperStock.com. **Page 5**:
PlusONE/Shutterstock.com; Chris Collins/
Shutterstock.com; George H.H. Huey/
SuperStock.com; Extreme Dominica.
Page 7: loneroc/Shutterstock.com;
Michael Runkel/SuperStock.com;
GIUGLIO Gil/SuperStock.com. **Page 8**:
Walter Bibikow/SuperStock.com.
Duotone Page 28: Travel Bug/
Shutterstock.com:

Printed in Spain by GraphyCems

Publishing information
Footprint St Lucia & Dominica
2nd edition
© Footprint Handbooks Ltd
October 2015

ISBN: 978 1 910120 56 9
CIP DATA: A catalogue record for this
book is available from the British Library

® Footprint Handbooks and the
Footprint mark are a registered
trademark of Footprint Handbooks Ltd

Published by Footprint
6 Riverside Court
Lower Bristol Road
Bath BA2 3DZ, UK
T +44 (0)1225 469141
F +44 (0)1225 469461
footprinttravelguides.com

Distributed in the USA by
National Book Network, Inc.

Every effort has been made to ensure
that the facts in this guidebook are
accurate. However, travellers should still
obtain advice from consulates, airlines,
etc about travel and visa requirements
before travelling. The authors and
publishers cannot accept responsibility
for any loss, injury or inconvenience
however caused.